YOU!
Branding Yourself for Success

Deondriea Cantrice

Way, Inc
Prosper, TX

Way, Inc

ISBN: 979-8-8689-2053-0

Dedication

This book is dedicated to my oldest brother Robert T. Harris, simply because he told me to dedicate the book to him. Love you!

*Remember, you don't need swag
when you know who YOU are!
~Deondriea Cantrice*

Table of Contents

What is Personal Branding?

Why is Personal Branding Essential?

How to Build Your Personal Brand?

Be Visible!

Social Media and Your Brand!

Rebranding

Be **YOU!**

What is Personal Branding?

Have you found yourself asking for a Kleenex rather than a facial tissue? Requesting a Band-Aid rather than a bandage? Kleenex, Band-Aid and several other companies have branded themselves so well that their names have become synonymous with the product that they sell and the experience that that expect their customers to have.

The biggest misconception about branding is people often confuse branding with marketing, and really don't know what branding exactly is. Branding is not a logo, promotional material or marketing. *Branding in itself is defined as a kind, grade, or to be recognized by a stamp, trademark, logo or tagline. It is to indelibly impress, a seal.*

Since the beginning of time, branding has played an essential role in the evolution of our society. Whether it was a mark to signify a tribe or owner on cattle, the seal of royalty on an official document, or the name of a celebrity to add validity, branding has moved from a primitive identifier to a well-recognized form of non-verbal, vital communication.

Branding transcends across language, professional, geographic, and social-economic barriers. Something as simple as a symbol, sign or logo can bridge communication between a producer and consumer, open doors, create revenue and conversely turn consumers away. It is important to understand that a logo is not a brand. The logo represents the brand. The logo is symbolic of what is felt or thought about the brand. When you see the logo of your favorite brands, you think of your experience or feeling about that brand.

As an employee or an entrepreneur, chances are you don't have a logo, but you DO have a personal brand. Your name and/or product is your personal brand. Building a personal brand is creating an experience or expectation that you want others to have or feel when he or she interacts with you.

It is important to establish, cultivate and maintain your own personal brand. Whether you realize it or not, you are already a brand but the question is: is your brand working for you or against you?

Remember the good ole days when hard work earned you a raise, promotion or recognition that you sought? I know I do! There was a time when stability and longevity mattered. Not anymore. Is it enough that you know your job? Today, knowing your job is barely enough to help you keep your job, much less advance beyond your current position.

Personal branding is establishing *a unique promise of value; it is to authenticate you in order to establish trust and distinction.* Branding is the campaign that is used to distinguish a person, company, product, service or work that can is easily recognized. A successful personal brand has a few significant components. It has a unique name, visual identity, and a distinctive value proposition. A personal brand is used to differentiate people, work or services from each other and to help create associations in the minds of end users which will lead to awareness, preference and ultimately the choice.

In short, the goal of personal branding is to establish a presence in the mind of the audience that you encounter or are trying to reach. Personal branding, much like a career in itself, is about making a full-time commitment to the journey of defining yourself as an expert in your profession or field of interest, and defining the manner in which you will assist others. A personal brand should simulate the total experience of a pleasant relationship between you and someone familiar with your admirable and unique qualities.

Write down the top 5 things you would expect others to experience. Ask a close friend that you trust to describe the most remarkable traits or experiences about having a relationship with you. Are your answers and your friend's answers the very different or similar? If they are similar, good for you! If not, there are some inconsistencies with your personal brand and you my friend have some work to do.

Personal branding is not just for the entrepreneur or c-level executive. It is for anyone that wishes to establish themselves with uniqueness in order to accomplish his or her goals, status, and ultimately achieve the individual success that he or she desires. Whether you are looking to move from clerk to CEO or sole proprietor to mogul, personal branding has to accompany your plan of action. It's your brand that will establish you as a subject matter expert in the workplace. It is your brand that will position you as an industry leader in the marketplace.

An interesting aspect of personal branding is that your brand can be inherited, developed, or formed as a result of your interactions with others. There are pros and cons with each approach to forming your personal brand. Even with an established brand it must be maintained and fostered. A personal brand, good or bad has staying power. People will always remember the experience, how they felt and its value or lack thereof.

Most people would love to have been born a Kennedy, Rockefeller or any other prominent name of an elite family. With any one of those well-known names, the descendants ultimately inherited not only a fortune and legacy, but they inherited their personal brand. The jury is still out on whether inheriting a brand is a good or bad thing. When a personal brand is inherited, all you have to do is maintain that brand. It is assumed that if you are a Kennedy, you are well versed in politics. The name itself is a brand that comes with inherent expectations of knowledge and a suggested career path.

The good news about inheriting a brand is the foundation has already been laid. All you have to do is hold onto the reigns and go along for the ride. The downside of inheriting a brand is that the expectation of quality and/or service has already been set and regardless of your experience, resources and education you are expected to exceed a predetermined level of success. And, there is no mercy if you don't have the intrinsic *know-how* to maintain the integrity of the brand that you inherited.

You don't have to be born into a rich or famous family to inherit a brand. You can inherit a personal brand simply because of the company you work for, the position you hold, where you received your education and of course with whom you associate. In some cases you inherit the brand of your predecessor, the "last person" that occupied the desk or job before you. We all have heard someone say the phrase, *"You have big shoes to fill."* Because you have inherited a personal brand with the new role, you will also be held to the same high expectations set by the person that held that position before you. When you acquire or allow a brand to be given to you, it can be damaging and deter you from reaching the goals that you desire.

Several years ago, I applied for a new position with the company that I worked for. Not only was I well qualified for the role, I was already performing some of the duties required for the job. I didn't get the job and I was disappointed, but what was hurtful was the reason why. My manager explained to me that I was too flexible and knowledgeable to assume the new role.

"Because I have great work acumen and performance I can't be promoted?" I thought. I couldn't believe that I was being punished for doing what I was paid to do in a professional manner. I presented the issue to my mentor and he said,

"The problem is that you have become the sixth man on the team, which means you are the *go to person.*"

Of course I didn't understand what that meant because it sure didn't sound like a bad thing. He went on to explain that I was the person to pick up the slack and to fill in as needed. To promote me to this particular position would leave gaps in too many areas. And, I performed well but I never fostered a niche skill.

I had to take a realistic look at my situation. I was a member of the marketing department, but I had been filling in for the executive secretary, the sales assistant, and supported other departments as needed. I thought I was building my personal brand as a leader and dedicated "team player" with very distinct career goals. Much to my dismay, I realized that I had been given a personal brand of an employee with no direction. I was willing to do the work without being properly compensated, happy as a member of the support staff, and not an employee with management aspirations. Because I consistently filled in, I became a fill in, rather than a valued asset. The repetition of my actions made my brand real, though it was not my intent.

Let me be clear, I'm not saying don't be flexible or accept special projects. What I am saying is find a balance and make sure what you are doing is in alignment with your desired career path. The most important lesson I learned was to speak up and make sure my manager was aware of my career path.

We all have goals but very few of us plan how we will reach those goals. My ambition was to be a leader in a management role, but I had boxed myself in the personal brand of being the ideal support person. I wasn't known as a meticulous accountant, sharp secretary, or ingenious marketing professional, I was *"the person that could help."*

What are people saying when they talk about you? Is it what you want them to say?

I never guessed that the initiative that I was taking at work was not synonymous with leadership. I assisted with many projects throughout the office and was essentially doing everything anyone requested of me, but I was mastering nothing. I had built the reputation of a person that could get the job done. When people thought of me, what came to their mind and out of their mouth was, *Oh she'll do it,* not *Deondriea is an expert at that.*

The experience my coworkers and managers had with me was that I would get it done, making my personal brand the best person to follow directives rather than the person to delegate. Ultimately, I had to leave the organization in order to advance my career. It was virtually impossible for me to rebrand myself or be compensated properly for my performance.

I will discuss building and transcending your personal brand in a later chapter because it requires a more in depth explanation and attention.

Your personal brand begins with knowing who you are as a person. Self-awareness is an essential cornerstone of building a personal brand. You won't know the value of what you provide if you don't know your worth.

I was facilitating a training session and I randomly asked the participants to name their best three attributes. Everyone that answered fell into one of two categories. Either they struggled to come up with the answer or they rendered a canned response of, "I'm reliable, creative, and I have great communication skills." This leads me to believe that most people don't know what their talents are or the value that they provide.

I asked the people that gave the canned response, what does "reliable" look like? I explained that they were hired to perform a specific job and they showed up every day and did that. Is that valuable? Will coming to work at your scheduled time and doing what is documented in the job description be enough to distinguish you from the other associates performing the same job? The answer is NO!

If you are going to have a canned answer make sure the reasoning behind your answer is unique to you and demonstrates the value that you provide. Instead of saying, *I'm reliable*, try using a statement similar to the following,

I have shown that I am reliable by providing quality deliverables before the anticipated deadline.

In the example above, reliable is the attribute but the value is in the benefit that others experienced as a result of a person being reliable. When a manager is looking to assign a new project he is going to think of an experience whether good or bad before a particular name comes to mind then he or she will usually choose someone based upon that experience. The thought would be *the last time we were in a crunch, this person came through for us and we won the contract.* The thought will not be *"Let me think, who is reliable?"* People have a tendency to remember past experiences and associate a name with that feeling.

Think about one of the product brands that you purchase religiously. Why do you buy that particular brand? An experience popped in your mind that led to your answer. The particular dishwashing liquid I buy it because somehow grease ended up on my favorite shirt and after watching a commercial about how it cuts grease, I decided to put a little of the dishwashing liquid on my shirt and the stain came out. I have been a loyal consumer ever since. Although other brands may be cheaper, a positive experience has kept me loyal.

Your personal brand should embody trust and positive memorable personal experiences with all of your interactions. As you maintain your brand integrity and your audience experiences are positive, people will become loyal to your personal brand.

Here is an exercise for you to start thinking about what makes your brand (you) valuable.

What are your strengths?

____

____

____

____

As you think about your strengths, understand that there is a difference between a strength and what you're good at. Anyone can be trained to do something, and with repetition, he or she can do it well. But that is not a strength. Your strength, is something that you intrinsically know how to do and can do it effortlessly.

For example, by trade I learned how to plan and manage events very well. You would think I was destined to be an event planner because I'm good at it. But it probably takes me double the time and effort to plan an event than someone whose strength is event planning.

How have you utilized these strengths?

____

____

____

____

What is the value of these strengths?

____

____

____

____

It is equally beneficial for you to know what your areas of improvement are. More importantly, are these skills you wish to improve on, or are they even worth the effort? It is crucial that you know this information about yourself in order to know what to delegate and what to develop in order to leverage your strengths to foster the value of your brand. It's a good idea to know your *hot buttons* or pet peeves that will set you off as well.

What are areas of improvement?

____

____

____

Are these areas important enough to strengthen? Why, or why not?

____

____

____

What are the internal/external barriers that challenge your brand/abilities?

____

____

____

____

What are your "hot buttons?"

____

____

____

____

In a nutshell your personal brand is your reputation and the reputation of the product that you produce. Your product is not limited to manufactured goods for sale. Your product could be a report, project, performance or event created or executed by you. Remember your personal brand is conveyed in every deliverable, action, dialogue, attire, and environment.

What do you want people to think about you?
vs.
What do people think about you?

The way we see ourselves and the way others see us may be different. To brand yourself means to create positive memorable experiences with everyone you encounter. When people think of you or your company what comes to their mind? What do they feel? What is the lasting impression?

In a subsequent chapter, I will address how to develop and foster your personal brand. In the meantime begin to think about why you buy or do business with certain brands. It will be easier to decide what your brand is and how to foster it when you can recognize what draws you to certain brands.

What characteristics describe you the person, YOUR work?

____

____

____

What makes you, your business, or your work unique?

____

____

____

What are your priorities?

____

____

____

____

What is your goal positioning?

____

____

____

____

If you are known for everything, you won't be known for anything! A personal brand is an authentic depiction of who you are, what skills you have acquired, and the value you continuously provide. Your brand helps you to get noticed and draw people to you. The appeal of your personal brand will determine whether someone will want to have a sustainable business relationship with you and tell others about you and the service or product that you provide.

NOTES

NOTES

Why is Personal Branding Essential?

Personal branding is no longer an option;
it's a powerful position conduit.

Have you defined your personal brand? Are you consistently living your personal brand every day? Your personal brand is not about what you say, it is what you provide. Unfortunately, personal branding has become a term that is used too loosely and has lost its intention. People have chosen to use the term "personal branding" irresponsibly to create visibility without relevancy, value or uniqueness. Developing a personal brand is a journey of self-exploration and continual development that extends far beyond popular notoriety.

Personal branding is more than a buzz phrase. I know you may not believe that branding yourself is worthwhile, but you are mistaken. By specializing in a niche skill set, you can gain the necessary visibility in order to achieve the financial reward, promotions, and the client/fan base that you desire. Developing your personal brand is essential for the advancement of your career and your ability to earn a fair compensation for the value that you bring to the organization.

Your personal brand is a tactical asset that assists you in creating loyal customers and advocates. If you don't believe branding works, look around your home or office and ask why did you choose a certain brand over another? The particular brands that you buy bring added value to your life in one aspect or another. It's important to understand that price and value are not synonymous. If an employer or client can see the value that you, your product or service provides, price sensitivity becomes obsolete. People are willing to pay a premium for a premium product or service.

Think of your personal brand as a trademark, an invaluable asset that you must protect while you continuously foster and maintain it. I hate to break it to you but, your personal brand is not an asset to make you look good or appear better. Your personal brand has to be managed with the intent of providing value to help others benefit from having a relationship with you and/or by being associated with your work.

Believe it or not, you are not the only person that provides the service or product that you do. In some cases, there may be someone that can even perform the task better than you. That is why it is important to know what your added value is. What is it that you bring to the table that compliments the objective or aligns with the vision or culture of your employer or clients? Take your time and think about that. If you have spent more than 30 seconds pondering an answer, you have not established a personal brand that others may not distinguish the value in.

The tools you used to get you to this level
may not get you to the next level!

Some of us can look back over our career and a pat on the back is warranted. You have been successful to this point either with intent or accident. You may have chartered your career path, or simply moved with the flow. But what you did to get you here, may not sustain you here or advance you to the next level.

Every day the marketplace and the workplace become more and more competitive. If you don't continue to increase your value, you will easily move from the leader of the pack to the bottom of the pile. You don't have to reinvent yourself, but you do have to remain relevant and valuable in order to maintain a position in the minds of those that are advocates of your brand.

There are major benefits in building your personal brand. It will establish you as a subject matter expert, it will promote consistency, and it builds trust. In building your personal brand you will be able to attract the clients, money and opportunities that you desire. Once you attract the people, you will have to convert them into loyal brand advocates.

Establishes you as a subject matter expert

We all have a plethora of things that we know how to do, can do, and are good at. But when asked, "What do you do?" and you answer, "*A little bit of everything.*" That tells me absolutely nothing. What you are good at or enjoy doing may not be your core competency. You have to provide a direct answer in order to create great results. It is vital that you develop a specialty to provide and foster.

At age 30, I still didn't know what I wanted to be when I grew up. I was so versatile in my talents that I had not honed in and became excellent at anything. Although I was an author, my personal brand was that I was a branding professional, life coach, social media expert, business coach or whatever people needed me to be in that moment.

One would think being versatile would give me the lion's share of the market. It didn't. I received very few referrals because my brand was not congruent with the experience that people had with me. My website reflected that I was an author, but I helped people with their branding efforts. When people visited my website and saw that I was a fiction writer, they didn't follow through with contacting me about their branding needs. If I was going to choose to be both a branding professional as well as an author, my marketing campaign needed to reflect both professions.

If you are uncertain about what you should specialize in, ask yourself what can you do that few others know how to do, and are willing to pay you to do it for them? When you possess a balance between your education and profession, life, and personal experiences, this is the foundation for determining what your niche is.

A benefit of having a personal brand is that when you have a clear understanding of who you are, what you do best, who you want to work with, and how you want to use your talents, you also know what you *don't* want in your life. Use your personal brand like a filter. It makes it easy to say no to opportunities that are outside of the scope of your brand, and easy to say yes to the right opportunities. By branding yourself, you gain the clarity to focus your energy on what's truly important to you.

Think of repeat business when you look to gain name recognition in your area of expertise. Ensure that your name leaves a lasting positive impression that sets you apart from the competition. To possess a great brand you not only have to be good, you have to be different in a way that will make people pay attention.

Aim for a small niche in your field and completely dominate it. Over time you will gain credibility, respect and even admiration when your name, which is your personal brand, is visible to your target audience. Increased visibility online and offline will promote your expert status and your strong brand will help you excel in your industry.

When you are the expert no one will question you because you speak with authority and trust.

In order to establish yourself as a subject matter expert, you have to do what you do consistently and do it with excellence. It is important to understand, know and love your craft. I used to work with a data analyst that most people within the organization didn't like because she was direct, firm but extremely efficient. Ok, direct and firm was the nicest way that I could say, rude and abrasive! I loved working with her because the reports she produced were always accurate, timely and easy to read. So when it came time to create a task force for a project that I was managing, I chose her to be a part of the team because I felt no one knew the data better than her or possessed her level of expertise. She was the data expert as far as I was concerned.

Promotes Consistency

The strength of a personal brand is measured by its consistency of delivery and relevance to consumers. The success of a brand strategy is contingent upon being consistent; ensuring that existing and potential audiences are familiar with and are interested in what the brand has to offer. Consumers expect consistency and a strong, sustainable brand that is known for its distinctiveness and defined set of qualities that are alluring to the audience and captivates their attention. When a brand is consistent and distinctive it will establish an image in consumers' minds that creates awareness within the target audience.

In order for your personal brand to remain significant to its audience, your brand must continually reinforce its value; build consciousness, and preference among its target audiences. When everything you produce has a common look and feel, the audience will be able to easily identify your brand.

It seems like every time we read the business section of the newspaper, a major corporation has gone out of business and is enduring a financial hardship. Why, when these corporations have been household names for years? Some people would argue the company's demise is a result of a poor business, marketing, or financial plan. In some cases that is true or at least partly true but if researched further, you will also discover that the company lost their brand identity.

The corporations that have remained sustainable during trying times are the companies that have been able to remain consistent and focus on their core competencies. Those businesses may have changed their methodology of delivery, but the message has remained the same. Consistency breeds trust because people know what to expect.

Building trust

Have you bought something because your favorite celebrity, best friend or some other influential person you know endorsed it? Most likely you didn't take the time to research it because you took the word of that person at face value because you trust them and their judgment.

By being visible and consistent, the audience will become more familiar with you and will begin to trust you and your opinion. This is important because people will be more apt to listen to you and refer you to others when trust is established. By establishing trust, it will potentially increase your business opportunities and generate more revenue for you.

If you provide value, people will want to follow and interact with you. But, you need to determine the type of people you want interacting with you. Not everyone is your customer. If you need direction, define your niche and focus only on that niche. People often look at their peers and see that their peers have become successful in a particular arena and automatically think *I can do that too*. Let that be a passing thought. When a person masters their niche skill, it will appear that what they do is easy and effortless. It's because they have mastered their craft. Stick to what you know and jump on the wave of the *next best thing*.

Comparing yourself to others is not the way to improve your personal brand or gain more clients. It is vital that you know who you are in order to know how you appear to others. Different is just different. Different is not better or worse. Strive for value. If you can show the benefit that you provide, most people will remain loyal to your brand, even if you are offering a similar product at an equal or a lesser cost. If you want to establish trust you have to deliver what you say you will deliver when you said you would deliver it.

Your target audience wants to know that you can provide what you say you're going to. Credibility is established by your actions, not your words. Your actions should align with and validate you as a brand that can be trusted and proves that you are credible. If you consistently live your personal brand and keep your brand promise to your target market, you will begin to establish reliability and trustworthiness.

NOTES

NOTES

NOTES

NOTES

How to Build Your Personal Brand

Throughout this book, I have discussed the foundation of personal branding. Now it's time to get to the meat of the matter, which is how to create, develop, foster and/or maintain your personal brand! The good thing about building your personal brand is the foundation is probably already laid and you can start from wherever you are. Whether you are an entrepreneur, an employee just beginning your career or somewhere in the middle, it's not too late to build your brand. If you somehow inherited a brand that you don't desire or aren't particularly fond of, here is your opportunity to rebrand yourself and achieve the success that you desire.

Remember it's your personal brand that will set you apart from others and keep you in the forefront of people's minds. It is important that you come up with a word that you are synonymous with. When creating a brand you should be able to offer one of three things: save someone money, make someone money or provide someone with an experience. Keep that in mind as you start to build your brand.

Your personal brand should represent the value you are able to consistently deliver to those whom you are serving. This doesn't mean self-promotion. You can create and foster brand awareness without always displaying your personal triumphs and success stories. Developing your personal brand requires you to be a great role model, mentor, and/or a voice that others can depend upon.

It is important that you know "what you want to be when you grow up." If you find that you are continuously "rebranding" yourself, you are uncertain of how you want to appear to the world. It's that uncertainty and inconsistency that will destroy your brand.

Stick to what you know, what you are good at, and what you desire to do. Now you may wear several hats, but they all should align with your brand. For example you may be a CPA that writes finance articles for a major trade publication, volunteer as the PTA treasurer, serve as an adjunct professor at the local community college, and during tax season prepare taxes.

As you can see, being a CPA allows you to perform a variety of roles, but all are a part of the brand. In theory you would most likely value a person skilled in one profession, but working in several arenas and industries.

Before you put the book down because you have experienced an ah-ha moment, it is important that you know I'm not saying to allow others or yourself to pigeon hole you a set career. You don't have to stay in the same industry or career your entire life. Remember, I said *branding is a unique promise of value*. If you've been everything from an airplane pilot to a stock broker, people will perceive that you have a problem staying focused and as a result your brand has become one of inconsistency and does not provide any value.

Being in the same line of work or the same industry and expanding or changing your career path is something totally different. If you are a customer service professional and decide to be a customer service trainer, that makes sense, because it's your experience as a customer service professional that will add the validity to your "know how." Also, if you have built a brand of a superior customer service professional, when people hear your name, they will say, "I hear he or she is the best in the customer service field."

The key element of building a successful personal brand is to remain consistent and adding additional skill sets. Too many changes will not only divert the attention of your audience, it may very well cost you the client or the job. Inconsistency causes confusion; you cannot expect people to remember what you are doing *now*. Continuous change makes it extremely difficult to build a solid reputation. How do you expect to maintain repeat customers and/or job stability when no one can give you a referral? It is difficult to perfect your craft if your craft is in constant change.

I attended an event where I met several people. I gave my business card to one lady in particular that didn't have a need for my services at that time. Almost a year later, I received an email from her inquiring about my services. What if I decided to do something different during that span of time? Do you think she would have been interested in my "new venture" or would she have contacted the next person that could provide her with what she needed? I would have shot myself in the foot if I had decided to abort my path to start a new journey. Evolving is always good, but a complete metamorphosis can be expensive.

It is virtually impossible to establish yourself as an expert if no one knows what you want to be "known for." Before you can begin to build your brand, it is important that you clearly define what you want to be or what service you want to provide, and its value. That will reduce the likelihood that you will have to rebrand yourself again and again.

A brand strategy details how the brand, its identity, product, packaging, services and experiences are associated and identified with a set of emotional and mental attributes such as brand image, values, associations, and unique selling points. The brand strategy defines how a brand is linked to a promise of value that consumers are willing to repeatedly purchase.

In order to build a successful brand, the tools and methods of how a brand communicates unique value and relevance must be identified and leveraged. This can only be accomplished once you identify who your ideal client is and what matters most to the person or organization.

A marketing strategy is the allocation of resources for a brand to be effective, given sales and marketing challenges or competitive activity. A brand strategy must come before the brand communications strategy, and it must be linked to future sales and growth. You have to know your value before you can effectively convey it to others.

Let's begin with a few questions to determine where you are and where you want to be. This will help in determining if you are headed in the right direction.

Has your brand/reputation been developed or did it happen?

____

____

____

____

If your personal brand has been given or inherited, no need to panic. Continue to answer the questions because your responses will prove useful when you get to the rebranding chapter. If you have made a conscious effort to build your brand, the next series of questions will help align your actions with your brand to ensure you are obtaining your desired results.

What are you passionate about?

____

____

____

What would you like your personal brand to be? *List three words that you would like to come to mind when clients and/or hiring managers hear your name or see your work?*

1. _______________________________________

2. _______________________________________

3. _______________________________________

What do you do? Or in some cases want to do? *You should be able to answer this question using 8 words or less. The more concise you are the more precise your plan of attack will be.*

____

____

____

You should be able to sum up what you do in 8 words or less. For example, *"I develop accounting software for small businesses."* Or, *"I create eMarketing solutions for published authors."* If you can't describe what you do or what you want to be known for in less than 8 words, it is virtually impossible to establish a brand identity.

What is it that you want to be known for?

____

____

____

Think of yourself as a corporation. All corporations have built a reputation for themselves and you choose to do business with them for that reason. Would you want to do business with someone that you weren't sure what they do, or how it is of value to you? Or, their explanation is so cumbersome that you forgot what the original question was?

If you have to explain what you do in an introduction, use a simple phrase such as *Top-Notch Sales Executive, Creative Strategist, Award-Winning Author*. Have your creative juices started to flow? What is your phrase?

Phrase: _______________________________________

If you don't know what you want to be known for, it is impossible for you to build your personal brand. You may land that big client or get the "right" job, but if you don't continue to foster your personal brand, you will find yourself pigeon-holed and consistently looking for ways to reinvent yourself. Then you will wake up asking yourself, "How did I get here?" or "Will something better come along?"

As a professional, an effective brand strategy must include advertising, point of sale and digital or direct marketing. Each of these disciplines must work both on their own and in concert to create an effective campaign for your brand. Even as an employee, you still need to fine tune these components to fit your career goals.

There is not a silver bullet to building your personal brand, but there is a recipe. Just like anything, add the tools to your tool box and use them when they are appropriate. You have to create an effective theme or series of messages related to your brand. When the theme or message is communicated to audiences an awareness, recognition, preference and ultimately choice for your brand will develop.

Visual Appearance

I can only imagine the big sigh that you took as you thought to yourself,

"Am I going to have to go shopping or become a contestant on a makeover reality show?"

Lucky for you, a shopping spree will not be necessary, unless of course you need an excuse to make a run to the nearest mall. Depending on your industry, position, age and status, what you wear will vary.

You probably have a wardrobe that consists of clothes for every occasion. But does your wardrobe reflect your personal brand? What do your clothes say about you? What are you saying to others before you even open your mouth?

The point is: Are you and your attire sending the same message about who you are? Are you reserved? Old fashioned? Fashion forward? Are you meticulous? Or flamboyant?

Depending on your age, industry, body type, position, personal preference and other varying factors will determine how you should dress. The only absolute is to dress how you want to be perceived.

How do you dress?

____

____

____

Why? Do you buy what's on the mannequin? Whatever is on sale? What other's wear? Or what you have always worn?

____

____

____

____

What image does your wardrobe represent about you to others? *Ask a few people that you trust to give you an honest answer. And no, "you always look cute" isn't an answer.*

____

____

____

A great way to determine if your attire represents your personal brand is to ask someone that you have recently met, have only been friends with or worked with for a short time. What did they think of you when they first met you? Give the people that you are asking permission to be honest. Be comfortable with the answer without offering an explanation of why you were wearing what you were wearing.

What do people think about you?

____

____

____

____

There is not a right or wrong way to dress. However, the rule of thumb is to dress in a way that mirrors your target audience. If you are looking for business investors for your accounting firm, it's probably not wise to wear a short sleeve shirt exposing your sleeve of explicit tattoos. Nor is it appropriate to wear a three piece suit and tie if you are meeting with farmers in a small town.

Although you have your own style, it is essential to "own your style." Comfort is key! If you aren't comfortable it will show through your body language. You can be you, while being appropriately dressed.

While growing up, my son hated wearing glasses. He thought they made him look like a "nerd" or a "square." When he grew up he realized that he absolutely needed glasses if he wanted to see and function. Knowing that wearing glasses was inevitable, he decided to make his spectacles the perfect wardrobe accessory.

My son bought multiple pairs of glasses that varied in designer brands and styles. What was once a thorn in his side has become a fashion statement and talking point! Once people started complimenting him on his glasses, he made them a part of his wardrobe and signature style.

The point I'm trying to make is it could be a single brand, color, accessory or style that reflects who you are. Also, that significant item will not only serve as a talking point but can be a conduit to getting your foot in the door.

Several years ago, I developed a keloid in the middle of my chest. The scar didn't bother me but it became a detractor in conversations because people would look at me and wonder what happened, if it was okay to ask me, and not pay attention to what I was saying. So, I decided to start wearing necklaces. These necklaces became my signature style. I was at an event one evening and a woman complimented me on my necklace several times. In fact she pointed it out to others. The next day I swung by the department store, picked one up for her and mailed it with a note that simply said,

"Now people are going to think we are twins. Have a great and amazing day."

She knew immediately who sent her this gift and she no doubt dug through the mountain of business cards that she collected in order to call me. From this small trinket, I was able to enter a door to a business relationship that may not have been accessible if I hadn't reached out.

Environment

What does your environment look like? I.e. desk, cubicle, office, car, etc.? I know you might be thinking, "Deondriea has gone off the deep end. My workspace and car have nothing to do with my personal brand?"

You are sadly mistaken. Just like your personal appearance, the area that you operate in is equally important and reflects your brand. Does your work area show that you are organized? Cluttered? Inviting?

It doesn't look good for a traveling salesman out making sales calls to have debris falling out of the vehicle when the door opens. Nor is it wise to have an office so sterile that people are too uncomfortable to sit down. Is your office overly saturated with personal awards and accolades, giving others the impression that you are more concerned about personal accomplishment than providing personal service?

Because humans are first and foremost visual beings, people will judge you by what they see around you. Although there is not a set standard of what your area should look like, it should reflect a balance of who you are and the image that you desire to portray. Do you want to project the image of being a family man? If so you may want pictures of your family or artwork created by your children in your office. If you want to project an image that is focused, be sure that there is order in your work area.

I strongly suggest that your work area, whether it is your car, cubicle, studio or office reflect the competencies that you present and the connector that exists between you and the clients that you service. You are human so it's ok to have personal effects around, but don't display anything that you do not want to explain and/or discuss. If you don't want to talk about your rock collection or religious beliefs don't display them in a business environment.

Elevator Speech

What if you stepped onto the elevator and pressed the button for the 18th floor, and just before the doors to the elevator shut, someone jumps into the elevator with you, and presses the button for the 16th floor? You immediately notice that the person that just stepped on the elevator with you is your ideal client, an investor, and stakeholder or decision maker. There you are alone for no more than 1 minute to sell yourself, idea, or service to that person. Are you ready? Earlier I mentioned that you have to "look" the part. Now the second piece is to present your brand.

An elevator speech is nothing more than a fast, concise summary of what you do and how it will benefit the person or audience that is being addressed. This pitch should be no more than 30 seconds. Of course this speech is not strictly reserved for elevators, but it should be executed as a sound bite to gain the interest and ultimately the business of a potential client. Here is a sample Elevator Speech:

"Hello my name is Jack Smith and I am a brand architect. I help entrepreneurs and small businesses increase their online reach through content development and execution in order to generate revenue and produce brand advocates."

As you can see that was straight to the point telling who, what and why. I have heard people say, *"It's hard to explain what I do."* Again, if you can't explain what you do in eight words or less, you may want to revisit your business plan and scale down the scope of what you do. Chances are if you can't easily explain it, a potential client won't be able to understand it, which will make it hard to get a yes.

There may be the desire to wing it or be spontaneous with your elevator speech. I don't recommend that approach. That moment has the potential to be a pivotal point in your life. This is not the time to go off the top of your head. It's a good idea to rehearse your elevator speech a few times. It wouldn't even hurt to practice it in the mirror. The reason preparation is essential is so that your key points are etched in your mind, which will decrease your chances of being caught off guard.

If you need assistance in developing your elevator speech, there are several templates that can be found online. It is a good idea to have a hard copy of your elevator speech to distribute as needed, in addition to the ability to recite it upon demand.

5/15

Many times people miss their opportunity for praise and promotion because they do not get the recognition that they deserve. It's not because they aren't valued or their manager is being malicious, it's because people lack the ability or willingness to promote and bring attention to themselves, or their work. You can't rely solely on your manager to remember what you've done the previous 12 months or your coworkers to sing the praises of your accomplishments.

Many of us were taught that it is poor etiquette to brag and/or talk about ourselves. In some arenas that still holds true. Though not in the workplace or in our businesses. It is important that you build and maintain a praise or kudos arsenal! Your 5/15 is a quick snapshot of what you have accomplished that contributes to the success of the stakeholder. The reason this is necessary is to keep what you are doing on the mind of the client, manager, or director.

Other than the major projects that you worked on, do you remember all of the company "wins" that you accomplished throughout the year? Chances are you don't and neither do the higher ups. It's not just the major accomplishments that matter. Believe it or not those little contributions do add up. Documenting those small wins shows the consistency of your contribution and demonstrates that YOU are an integral team member.

There are several beneficial reasons to maintain a 5/15 log. Keeping record of your major accomplishments and minor milestones will assist you in securing a better performance review that may result in a higher salary increase. It could also be a tool used to negotiate a contract because clients and employers alike, desire to see what is the added value that you are able contribute. Some of the information in the 5/15 can also be used to develop content for your sales proposal.

The 5/15 is not just for the employee. As an entrepreneur or if you are self-employed, your 5/15 may include client testimonials and other information that a potential client may deem useful. For example, if you are a real estate broker you may add that one of the houses you listed sold within two weeks of being on the market or you were able to get a client $10k more above the asking price. Do you see the difference that it will make to have at your fingertips concrete captions of the value you bring to your client? Your 5/15 will be quite useful; you can repurpose this information in your newsletter or online communications. Also, it will help distinguish you from the other people that provide the same products or services that you do.

This praise arsenal is referred to as a 5/15 because it should take you a maximum of 15 minutes to write and 5 minutes for the person reading it to review. It's up to you if you update your 5/15 on a daily, weekly, monthly or quarterly basis. Your updates should correspond with your industry and position. Do not try to rely on your memory. Even if you don't present your 5/15 to anyone immediately, update it as often as you are able to. Focus on your successes, accomplishments, and never discount your value by downplaying a particular win or doubt yourself by over analyzing why or how you handled a particular situation.

Again, this is a document that you own so share it at will with whomever you desire to ensure that you receive the recognition for your contributions. Be proud of your accomplishments and know when to share them and with whom. You can choose to document it and not share until it's time for your annual performance review. What's important is that you stand proud, without being overly critical or too analytical about what you have achieved. You are on stage and this is your opportunity to shine!

It takes time to build a brand and develop brand advocates. Brand integrity is vital! Potential clients and employers need to be able to identify you and your work. Maintaining brand consistency is the foundation necessary to build a lasting brand.

Building your brand doesn't have to be some cumbersome process. There are a few key elements to keep in mind when building and fostering your personal brand.

1. *Clarity*-Create a message that is concise and to the point. Your audience should know exactly what your brand represents and the value it brings.

2. *Delivery*-Don't offer a promise of value that you cannot deliver. Clients expect a quality deliverable in a timely manner.

3. *Identity*-Create a brand that your audience will recognize and identify.

4. *Continuity*-Your audience will develop loyalty to brands that have staying power.

Your specific needs, industry and resources will determine the strategy that will help build and foster your brand. You may use all, some or a variety of the options at various times. What's important is that your message remains consistent. If you change your message, you may lose credibility with the people who are loyal to you and your brand. The goal is to influence people to connect with your product, respect and recognize it. It is important to remain visible. I have dedicated the entire next chapter to brand visibility.

NOTES

NOTES

NOTES

Be Visible

How can you be found if no one knows that you exist? In today's ever changing world, it is easy to get lost in the shuffle or the wave of a viral trend. It is common to be overlooked because of an administrative error or simply forgotten because you didn't leave a lasting impression. Your personal brand (your name and/or work) should be on the forefront of the minds of the people that you are trying to reach even when you are not physically present. In building your personal brand, it is important to be and stay visible! It is important to find a place to occupy in the minds of the people you are trying to reach. Understand that seeking attention is not the same as being visible.

Let me be very clear. Do not be obnoxious or develop what I consider to be the *eager puppy syndrome*. The eager puppy syndrome is when a person bounces from one activity, cause, clique, company, or conversation to another without reason, invitation or interest. When a person acts like the eager puppy, it is perceived that they are chasing everything and focusing on nothing. If you appear at inopportune times and places, inserting yourself inappropriately, you will be given the brand of a pest. People will deem you as unfocused and assume you are waiting for the next wave of events or "big thing." Employers, fans, and potential clients will assume that you lack loyalty and view you, your work, and/or service as temporal. It is vital to be strategic with your appearances and input. When you have value and are visible you won't have to chase opportunities, they will find you.

Personally, I found the quieter that I became, the more I learned, the more focused and strategic I became. By being quiet or still, I was able to identify who I wanted to attract and how to attract them. You can't expect to be successful hunting if you don't have the right bait. I have been known to attend events for the first time and blend into the wall the best way that I knew how. By doing that I was able to gather information that was necessary for achieving my goal. You will be surprised how quickly you learn what NOT to do in your approach.

Ultimately, find a way to be unforgettable without being obnoxious. People should be excited to see you come, not thankful to see you go.

There are several ways that you can promote yourself and make your brand visible without being obnoxious, narcissistic, or appearing as an opportunist. Let's explore a few of these options to make your brand visible.

Volunteer/Participate

I know that you are expecting me to say something profound like volunteering is fulfilling, rewarding, and it is your responsible service to society. Although those intrinsic feelings are true and everyone should volunteer in some capacity or another, volunteerism is also a no cost/low cost way to be visible and build or maintain your brand identity. When you volunteer you make your brand visible and in some cases improve your skill set and/or the quality of your deliverables.

Before you take off running to pick up your volunteer badge, it is important to understand why, when and with whom you should volunteer. In building your personal brand, you have to be methodical and understand the *whys* and *whats* to volunteering. What are you willing to give? And, what do you desire to gain? Volunteering just because is not a valid reason. If you don't understand why you are doing something, the importance of it and how it benefits you, it will become a disaster waiting to happen.

Today many companies promote and take pride in their social responsibility. On the website of most corporations, you will find information about the company's philosophy and evidence of their philanthropic views and engagements. In fact, a lot of companies list their corporate sponsorship requirements right on their website. In some instances, companies have a department or task force dedicated solely to volunteering and sponsorship. This is not just about charity; it's about remaining "visible" in the communities they live and conduct business in. Corporations see the mutual benefits in volunteering and so should you.

It only makes sense that you research volunteer opportunities to discover which ones suit you and which community service events are gateways to that company and/or clientele that you are trying to build a relationship with. By no means am I saying volunteer with an agenda. But, what I am saying is, volunteer with purpose. If someone asks you why you are volunteering, no answer or a canned response can damage your brand.

There are a number of benefits to volunteering. Volunteering shows that you are socially conscious and willing to invest in what you believe. It is also an excellent way to grasp the attention of stakeholders, potential clients and/or future business prospects. Having a common interest with an organization or person makes it easier to communicate, partner with, sell to and/or provide exposure. Don't run out and join every committee and soup kitchen. People will notice very quickly if you are disingenuous. More is not always better.

Volunteer for the events and causes that align with your personal brand, product, beliefs, and/or goals. For example, if you enjoy planning parties and family events on the weekends you may consider volunteering for the employee picnic or annual holiday committee. This will give you the opportunity to do something that you enjoy, show that you know the company culture, and interact with people in departments that you may not normally come in contact with. This concept works the same if you are a business owner. Volunteer or sponsor the community events that align with your skill level and interest. How you volunteer is equally as important as where you volunteer.

If you have children, volunteer at one of their school activities. Again, let me stress that you should volunteer to do what you enjoy and/or have the skills to do. If you don't enjoy cooking, don't sign up to bring desserts to the bake sale. Instead, sign up to be the cashier, help with the marketing, organizing, or be a part of the cleanup crew. Just as you are a professional, the parents of your children's classmates are too. A sidebar conversation may very well lead to your next opportunity.

It's important not to volunteer so much that you neglect your personal and professional responsibilities. Don't volunteer to the extent that your health, family, work or finances suffer. Let your time and other resources dictate how you choose to donate your services.

When you volunteer to do what you enjoy or have the skill set to do, you will become actively engaged in the activity, committee, or event that you signed up for. Do not sign up, miss the meeting and fail to follow through on your commitments. If you cannot volunteer your time, make a donation or purchase an ad whenever it's available. It never hurts to have your name or logo in a souvenir book, on a t-shirt, or announced when the sponsors, contributors or volunteers are recognized.

We all know that volunteering is an opportunity to make a difference in our communities and as we already discussed, it is also a way to promote our personal brand. Volunteering is also a great way to extend your network; it will allow you to connect with potential employers, clients and/or partners.

One afternoon, a couple of my employees and I were volunteering at an annual event for our local Chamber of Commerce. During a passive conversation with another volunteer, a woman asked how I found my two new hires that were with me because she has had a difficult time filling a position within her organization. She briefly explained the position to me. I told her my new hires were internal candidates but I knew of a person that would be a great fit for her position. I wrote my friend's name and number on the back of my business card, took the woman's business card and said, "I will give her your contact information as well." Long story short, just a couple of weeks later my friend was hired, and I received a thank you card with two tickets to a major sporting event with excellent seats. I in turn used the tickets to treat a potential client.

As you can see, volunteering turned out to be beneficial for everyone involved. The charity received the help it needed, I made a connection, my unemployed friend got a job, and the woman's company acquired a great new employee. Did you notice what I did? Rather than simply taking her card, I gave her my friend's contact information on the back of my business card. My card was not just a way of keeping my contact information at her fingertips; it also served as a "reference," for lack of a better term, for the candidate (my friend).

I know you may think, "All this is good information but it's not really applicable to me because I'm not looking to leave my current employer." The good news is if community service is not your "thing" you still have an opportunity to volunteer and build your brand within your organization.

Many of us have a story about how someone got a promotion that everyone knew the person didn't deserve, and wondered how or why they were promoted over others. Well, most likely this person volunteered for special projects or for various committees. Holiday parties are usually pretty cheesy and let's face it, how many brats and burgers can you endure year after year at the company picnic? Volunteering on a committee or task force at your company allows you to be visible and to expose you to other departments and hiring managers that you may normally never come in contact with.

Taking on those additional tasks gives you the opportunity to *strut* your stuff, prove that you are a self-starter, a person that takes initiative and works well with others. Volunteering on a special project also displays your ability to be flexible and to collaborate effectively with other work groups. More importantly you have proved that you have added value to the organization. Now you know why that other person that may have been equally or less qualified than you received the promotion. Believe me when I tell you, volunteering is more effective than brown-nosing. But it won't hurt to continue to laugh at your boss' corny jokes.

Don't feel like your community service or volunteerism isn't genuine if you have a purpose or objective in mind? With hundreds of thousands of charities available, and new 501c(3)s forming daily, there has to be a method of choice.

Corporations usually sponsor causes that are in alignment with the product or service that the corporation provides. Or they sponsor a cause that is near and dear to the heart of the decision maker(s). Meaning, you will usually see kid's products sponsor kid events or the company sponsors MS, breast cancer or diabetes because one of the C-level executives has a friend or family member that suffers from one of the previously mentioned illnesses.

Serving the community by volunteering at a school, soup kitchen or 5k walk may not be your thing, *don't force it!* There is still a way that you can "be visible" through volunteerism. Serving on a Board is included under the volunteerism umbrella.

There are board seats available with most major charities, city, county and state agencies. You are able to serve as a public or professional member depending on the board. A *professional board* member is defined as someone that is currently licensed and/or working in the specified industry or field related to the board. For example, a psychologist serving on the Psychologist Examiners Board is considered as a professional member. A *public member* is a member of the board without an association to psychology. Typically you will find a mixture of professional and public members on boards that are a part of a government agency. This is designed to protect the interest of the general public.

Serving on a board will allow you to collaborate with other professionals, sometimes from a variety of industries to make decisions that are best for the charity or organization. If you review the bio of most executives, you will find that they currently serve on a board, or have in the past.

Unlike passing out water, t-shirts or lanyards after a 5k run/walk, serving on a board requires true interest and dedication. Not to dismiss the role of a volunteer at a run/walk, what I'm saying is that committing to 2-6 hours on an annual basis is different than being a decision maker on a board that meets weekly or monthly. This leads to my next point.

There are several factors to consider when researching a board. First determine your commitment level. Do you have a job that allows you to attend board meetings during business hours? What is your evening and weekend flexibility? How frequently would you be able to attend meetings? Are you willing to fulfill tasks between meetings? These are questions you need to know prior to applying. If you are seeking a board position to pad your resume, that is your option. But, be sure you don't apply to an active board. Active boards may ask you to fulfill tasks between meetings, such as subcommittee meetings, readings and attending events to name just a few.

Every board will vary in requirements, seats and meeting schedules. However, most boards will require an application and/or interview. Be sure you know the expectations, mission, deadlines and requirements for the board before you apply. It's important to discover if the board has vacancies. Do not apply without conducting research first.

There are several ways to find out which boards are accepting applicants. Of course the internet is a great source of information. Use your search engine to search board vacancies. You can visit the agency's or company's website.

Ask your friends that are currently serving on a board that interests you if they have any vacancies. I can't stress it enough; make sure you have the interest and availability before applying for a board position.

Again, volunteer for things that will display you and your skills in the best light. Or volunteer with a cause that you truly believe in. The more passionate you are about a cause, the more committed you will be and the better you will perform. Your time is valuable, use it wisely and where you will have the most impact.

What community services interest you?

____

____

____

____

What are your personal priorities?

____

____

____

What are your business priorities?

____

____

____

____

Mentor/Promote Others

I know it seems like an oxymoron that promoting and/or mentoring others is a way of building your personal brand and promoting yourself in the process. It sounds very contradictory. Remember at the beginning of the book I said your brand is inherited, given or developed. It also transcends.

When you mentor and/or promote others, it gives you visibility without you having to promote yourself. When the person that you are mentoring and/or promoting is successful, people will value your recommendations establishing you as a trusted source. That is the reason that you would be aware of the people that you recommend and why. Your dear friend may own a catering business and you know that he doesn't have a professional work ethic don't refer him because you are his friend and you are trying to help him out. When he fails it will reflect on your negatively.

Many of us have watched a fight scene in a movie and the fight comes to a gridlock. One of the opponents asks the other, "Were you trained by Master Example?" The challenger nods, and the fight usually comes to an end at that point. A master fighter taught a pupil how to fight and the opponent was able to distinguish the fighting style or technique of the Master.

Let's bring it closer to home. Have you ever shared information or produced a quality deliverable and you were asked, "Who taught you how to do that? Where did you learn how to do that? How do you know this?" More often than not, your answer will be linked back to a mentor, teacher or experience. The methodology, language, mannerisms and other visible attributes reflect the brand of the person you acquired those skills from.

The evidence of your brand is transcended. When you develop a specialized skill set, or how you do what you, and it is fostered within someone you have mentored, their success and accomplishments promote your brand. It is an honor when a person can say that they have been trained by the best and that best is you. That is how a brand transcends.

We all believe in karma in one form or another. When we promote others, in turn others will promote us. This is not a game of *wash my back and I will wash yours*. The people that you promote most likely will not be the people that promote you. But, you've sown a seed of support and expect support as your harvest.

Continuing Education

The benefit of continuing education is two-fold. It is safe to say that learning is mentally stimulating, but it will also increase the value of your personal brand. The more you know, the more you will have to offer. The more you have to offer, the more people will be willing to pay and/or invest. We all need to be continuously cultivated and the people we interact with need to know that our knowledge base is not antiquated.

Knowledge is truly the greatest asset that a person can possess. Believe it or not, it is more valuable than money. Having knowledge will allow you to make money, but lack of knowledge may cost you money, time, and opportunities. More importantly, knowledge is the one asset no one can ever steal from you. You are the 100% vested, sole owner of what you know!

If the average person looks back into their childhood, he or she can probably remember someone telling them about the importance of school and urging them to go on to college. Most of us did what our parents told us to do. We went to school and in some cases, continued on to college or trade school. Now what? Are we supposed to stop learning once we graduate from formal education? The answer is NO! I would argue that real learning begins at the end of formal education. A grade point average proves that you were able to learn. Application is proof of what you have learned.

Continuing education does not always refer to college-credit coursework at a trade school or traditional college. Continuing education is training, self-education and/or certification acquired after traditional, formal education has ended. Continuing education includes and is not limited to conferences, workshops, reading material, licensures, and all other types of learning activities.

Are you stuck in a career holding pattern? Feeling like you are wasting away because you are bored or feeling complacent? Take a look at your career path. Are you where you want to be or have you left your career in the hands of the higher ups? If you have answered yes, then that means you have become a victim of letting your personal brand create itself. You are most likely deemed as a person with no ambition, with no desire to move beyond your current role, or maybe you have gone unnoticed. When was the last time you learned a new skill or certified a current skill?

Successful people consider learning as an investment in them, their deliverables and yes their personal brand! Continuing education is essential to reach and maintain a certain level of success. Even if the core competency remains the same, continuing education will teach you how to repurpose or diversify the knowledge that you have.

There are people that believe learning is a never-ending process. Those are the people that crave knowledge and information. Then there are those who understand the correlation between education, promotions and salary increases. Continuing education forces professionals to enhance their skills, not just to retain their current jobs, but also to improve their chances of career advancement, job retention as well as increasing their ability to be hired if they lose their current employment.

By taking advantage of advanced degrees or continuing education opportunities in your field, you will improve your chances of climbing up the corporate ladder and increasing your salary. If you are self-employed, continuing education will help you remain current and provide additional credentials. Would you hire a dentist or a lawyer that hasn't had any additional training since he or she graduated from school 20 years ago? Let's be honest, we are leery of places that haven't remodeled or upgraded within a certain period of time. Surely, we don't trust professionals that haven't updated their skills either.

The same goes for our education, it has to be upgraded, fine-tuned or serviced during the course of our life. Some adults pursue education because they have a hunger for learning. For them, education is a lifelong quest. These are people with inquisitive minds who have an insatiable appetite for "knowing more." Some people will pursue degree programs related to their professions, while others choose fields that they are interested in which may or may not be related to their professions. These are the people who need to be in the know.

For some, the reasons for continuing education have nothing to do with learning or earning. These people seek recognition or status to improve their image amongst friends and family. There is nothing wrong with having multiple degrees or initials behind your name. The key is in knowing the value of what those credentials bring.

There are several reasons why adults choose to pursue continuing education. No matter what the reasons are, the benefits are the same. It never hurts to know more. Continuing education will only add to a person's ability to be promoted or hired.

Continuing education will help build your personal brand because it will increase your knowledge, keep your skill sets current, and validate your credentials. Also, it will teach you new ways to utilize the tools you already possess. Tools have to be maintained and so should our education and skills. Every now and then, it is important that you assess your skills and determine how they can prove to be valuable. If you find yourself out of work, this is the ideal time to learn a new skill or improve your craft.

Overall, continuing education is going to be dictated by your industry, learning style, time and money. Some industries may require that you take specialized continuing education courses to maintain your licensure or designation while others may not.

Trade Associations/Organizations

Building your personal brand through trade organizations has a threefold benefit. It not only makes you visible, it also will help you be aware of what is going on in your industry, and it will position you to receive referrals or partnerships. When you can say that you are a *member of* a respected trade organization, it gives credibility to your brand.

Attending trade association events creates visibility for you, by exposing you to senior level staff that may be looking to hire. Trade organization events are great places to source for new talent as well. A room full of your peers is an excellent place to gain industry news and share information.

Trade organizations can be a breeding ground for referrals. By attending the various meetings and networking events your brand is present and should be top of mind when your constituents need to refer their clientele to someone. Even though you are in the same industry, your target markets may be different. Or, the company is overwhelmed and needs someone they can trust to send their clients to, because it's their brand that is on the line.

There are several ways to create or maintain your brand within your specific industry. Whether it's an association, workshop, tradeshow or networking event, there are sponsorship, speaking, and networking opportunities. The spot in the front of the room may not happen immediately, but at least you are in the room.

As a member of an association, your name and/or business will appear on directories and lists. This will make it easy for people to locate you. Usually within trade associations there is some type of industry publication. You may have an opportunity to pen an article, be featured, or place an advertisement. Just like anything else, you will get out of your experience what you put into it and expect from it.

Networking

I know the very term "networking" can make the hair on the back of your neck stand up and cause you to cringe in disgust. We all have our networking nightmares, but it is a necessary evil. Most people shy away from networking events because they are usually not worth the time and by far more trouble than the event is worth.

I have experienced more than my fair share of people sprinting across the room to pass out business cards like their life depended on it, and greeted me with that famous question, *"What do you do?"* Let's not forget the cheesy guy with the bad comb-over and overbearing, cheap smelling cologne. Or, the divorcee that is scantily clad seeking her prey. My all-time favorite is the pretentious salesmen that over talks everyone as he pats himself on the back and pitches his get rich scheme.

If the scene I just depicted reminded you of why you stopped "networking" let me assure you that is NOT what networking is all about. Networking *is the exchange of information and resources between people of similar interests and involves establishing relationships.* I could draft a complete book of the do's and don'ts of networking, but I will leave that to the subject matter experts. I will only address networking and your personal brand.

To foster your personal brand through networking, the key to success is building relationships. Building relationships by networking can lead to lucrative business ventures by way of referrals, promotions, partnerships and more.

In order to promote your personal brand while networking, you have to talk to people about what their needs, values, and challenges are. Just because they may not need your goods or services today, that doesn't mean that they won't ever need them or refer others. The mistake several professionals make is they only want to do business with people that do business with them in the moment. That is not networking; at that point you are selling.

You should pay attention to everyone, even if they don't look like your ideal client. I met a real estate broker at a networking event. I was not in the market to buy a home, but he was looking for someone to assist with marketing his business. Although I didn't buy a house he still hired me. After the marketing assignment was complete, he was no longer a client, but he was a part of my network. A few years later, someone I knew was looking to sell her home. Without hesitation, I referred her to that broker because he was top of mind. What if he chose not to hire me because I didn't buy a home? He probably would not have been a member of my network and would not have come to mind when it came to giving a referral.

Get to know all the businesses in your area and build a sustainable network of people that will support your brand. If you are a graphic designer you may want to know who the printers are. If you are a realtor you should know lenders. This will increase your potential for referrals and partnerships.

Never assume that a person cannot do anything for you especially based on his or her title.

There is a fallacy that you can be a one (wo)man show. When you build an effective network, you will be able to focus on the core competencies of your brand. You may need a CPA who doesn't have a use for your service, but he very well may have customers that do or will need your products or services. Never discount a person or their worth. A word to the wise, most administrative staff members are the gatekeepers to the executives. In some cases they are influencers to the decision maker that you are trying to reach. The key is build relationships with people not titles.

Several years ago I attended a networking event, of course met several people, and one gentleman actually followed up with me. As a result of that interaction, I granted him a $60k contract with my organization and eventually contracted him to do some personal business for me as well. A few months later, I was attending the same event where a guy observed us speaking and later asked the gentleman that won my contract why was he talking to me because I was "just an admin." The gentleman I had worked with told the guy that despite my title, I was responsible for a $1M advertising and promotional budget. Needless to say the guy made a beeline towards me and immediately tried to sell me his services.

This guy assumed that I couldn't do anything for him solely based on my title, instead of asking questions to build a rapport. I will say yes, the guy provided a service that I needed, but because he discounted me from our first interaction, I refused to do business with him.

Have a game plan

Our emails are bombarded with invitations from people to attend their event. How do you make heads or tails of the invite and which ones to attend? Your time is one of your most valuable assets so it's important to use it wisely. Before I decide which events to attend, I consider what my objectives are.

- Do I want to connect with someone in a specific industry?
- Do I just want to meet people because I'm new in town?
- Am I going to meet at least 5 prospects?
- Am I going to scout the competition?
- Or, am I going with the intent to meet the keynote speaker or other prominent person in the room?

- Do you want to cross pollinate with someone?

Once you are able to answer those questions, deciding which event(s) to attend will be easy. If you don't know why you're there, then how can you gauge if it was the best use of your time and resources? Don't be afraid to do your due diligence. Ask the host prior to the event what is the average number of attendees, age range and some of the industries that will be represented. It's important to show up with a plan of what you expect to gain or who you expect to meet.

After you decide what you expect to get from networking, decide how often you want to attend these events. Do you want to go to one a month, a quarter or a week? It is possible to oversaturate the event, meaning you have met everyone that you choose to meet.

Despite popular opinion, there are events used to network other than traditional "networking and/or mixers" events. Open houses, release parties, wine tastings and so on. Whenever you have the opportunity to meet and connect with people it is a networking opportunity.

It's a good idea to know what you want to talk about at these networking opportunities and a good idea to rehearse your introduction to make sure you don't sound "salesy." It's not even a bad thing to draft a couple of mental conversation starters. Choose things that are comfortable for you and plan your delivery. It's easy to break the ice and have small talk when you bring up the topic and feel comfortable sharing it. The exchange of small talk will help you find common ground with the person and begin to build that rapport. And, it will also equip you with information that you can later use as sales tools.

Small talk will help you find out if the person is a vegan versus a steak lover, what are their pain points and more. I know you are thinking, "How are you supposed to find out their interests in a buffet line or at the bar without tackling the person to the ground?" It's very easy, just listen and watch. If the person is constantly fidgeting with his or her smartphone that would indicate that they are a mobile person.

Networking is about connecting with people to extend your reach not to carry others along. Who you choose to network with and build relationships with represents your brand. Nurturing strong relationships with those who are most likely to speak on your behalf can be beneficial when you need someone to be your evangelist and vouch for your strengths.

Let's stay together

I never understood why people attend networking events, collect business cards, and then never follow up with the people they meet. Is there a secret society of business cards collectors that I don't know about? If you took the time to meet them, engage in conversation, don't you want to know what comes next. I know that you probably received a couple business cards from people you know you will never do business with and that is okay. But don't automatically add them to your mailing list without following up or at the very least asking them for permission.

A network is a support system birthed from relationships. It's wise to do favors for people in your network before you need their support. The gentleman that prints the bulk of my promotional material asked me to help him join cyberspace by launching his online presence. I did it as a favor for him and several months later he returned the favor by writing a testimonial for me and gave me a 50% discount on my next print job. My relationship with my printer is one that is mutually beneficial. We respect each other's time and craft.

Not every relationship in your network will be mutually beneficial, what's important is to know who to do a favor for and when. You have to know what you are willing to give, its value and what you stand to gain.

I was approached by a gentleman that asked if I would create a social media campaign for his business free of charge and in return he would post a link about my books on his website. I was immediately turned off with the fact that he asked for what he wanted, gave what he thought was a fair price and what he thought I needed in return. You guessed correctly, I said no. Here is the reason. If you choose to barter, it has to be an equitable exchange. This gentlemen and I had different target markets. He would have benefited from my services; however, I would have gained absolutely nothing.

You don't have to count cards. Better yet, don't give with the expectation of receiving from that person and don't give more than what you are comfortable giving. There is a difference between giving and investing. I don't believe in giving just because. When I volunteer or donate it's because I believe in the person, organization and/or what they are doing and I consider that an investment. For people in my network that I have relationships with, I give with gladness and don't expect it to be reciprocated.

Lastly, when you show up to network, you can reach the person that you are trying to reach by engaging others that are connected to him or her. There is no need to be among the barrage of people asking for a card and pitching themselves. You can remain visible by conversing with others. Be yourself and you will find that you will ultimately be introduced to that key person.

Promotion Material

Although this section will be geared towards the entrepreneurs/business owners, as an individual you will be able to grasp a few concepts for your personal branding tool belt as well. Your "promotional material" is how you deliver your services. What do your reports and presentations look like? How do you present your work for review?

What are your tools and packaging?

Promotional material has several benefits. It obviously promotes your brand, but it gives your brand an identity, and it provides people with a sense of belonging. When a person is an advocate of a brand, they wear the logo with a badge of honor. A brand's logo is also categorized with status, whether that status is unique and exclusive or part of the mainstream trend. This is why maintaining brand integrity is so essential.

I know you may be tired of hearing it, but it's important that if you don't get anything else from this book, you grasp the importance of consistency. I know this is an embarrassingly simple concept, but so many people have no idea the impact and power that consistency has. Your brand is built through repetition.

Let me start with your promotional material, specifically your printed items. All your printed material must match each other in terms of design, color and contain your contact information. Printing can be a costly expense, but under no circumstances should you cut any corners! Think of promotional material not as an expense but as an investment. A business card, stationary, or other printed material will determine whether others deem you as a professional or not. Also we interact with hundreds of people a day, how is anyone supposed to remember who you are and what you do?

I know social media has become the way to connect and keep in touch, but if your name is common a person may not be able to find you. Conversely, if your name is too unique a person may not know how to spell it. Why run the risk? You should make it easy for people to communicate with you. And, let's not forget that everyone has a preferred communication style and social media may not be it.

There are few things that you may want to consider when designing your promotional material. Choose a logo and colors that are professional, visually appealing, have longevity and reflect your brand.

When you work with a graphic designer to create your logo, what do you want the logo to say? Your logo should be the visual representation of your brand's story. Does the logo represent your brand? Is it eye catching? A logo should be clean. Think about the logos of your favorite brands, simple aren't they. It's ok to be clever but not overly creative with the design. Close your eyes and imagine looking at your logo from the 50 yard line at half-time during a football game. How will it look? What will people feel when they see it? If you don't believe logos are important, the next time you are driving down the highway, notice that the signs have the logos of stores and restaurants, not the names spelled out.

The stationary that you choose should have your logo and contact information on it. Whether it is an invoice, a letterhead or a flyer, make sure everything has a common look and feel.

If you are self-employed or an entrepreneur, it is a good idea to invest in promotional material such as pens, bookmarks, magnets, cups etc. as giveaways. Even if that person does not buy your goods or services, that cup with your logo on it may catch the eye of someone in their office, school or other event. When purchasing promotional material, try to avoid disposable items like candy, water or things that have a single use because the person will use and discard the item along with your contact information. However, a pen, bottle opener or hat will stick around for a while.

When making a decision to purchase promotional material, it is important to know your audience and whether what you are giving away aligns with your brand and/or activities that you are involved in. If you are a golfer or golf is the hobby of your target market you may think about putting your logo on golf balls or tees. If your business is dealing with health or wellness, your logo on a bottle of sanitizer can go further than putting your logo on bottle openers.

There is not a one size fits all kit for promotional material. You have to know what your target audience likes and work with that. Also, don't be afraid the use different promotional material at different events or at varied times. As an author, I give away bookmarks when I'm at a book signing, but if I am giving a speech or facilitating a class, I give away more expensive promotional materials like chapstick, notepads, or t-shirts. No matter what you decide make sure it aligns with your brand, audience and most of all, your marketing plan.

Remember promotional material is a gift that you are sharing. So make sure it's something people are excited to receive and not looking to re-gift. A graphic designer will help you tweak the design as needed for the different mediums.

Biography/Profile/Resume

The purpose of a Biography, more commonly referred to as a "bio," is a snapshot or executive summary of who you are, what you have accomplished, and what matters to you. In general, your bio should be no more than a single page long and should be a balance of who you are personally and professionally.

What value do you bring? i.e. experiences, connections, track record, and attributes?

____

____

____

____

____

An author contracted me to help her with marketing her book. In the process of gathering information for her marketing plan, I researched her online. Everywhere I looked, her bio read differently. Not only was it different, it was contradictory.

The author's book was about surviving domestic violence. One of her bios mentioned that her husband abandoned her and their marriage. But another bio read that she escaped domestic violence through the support of her family and friends. Without knowing her story, you would ask yourself what is the truth? What really happened? This minor discrepancy challenged her credibility and the validity of her experience. Was she really a battered wife, or was she writing about a "hot topic?"

I asked her about what I read. She explained to me that she packed up her kids, what she could carry and moved away. After which she never heard from him again and was granted a divorce based on abandonment. As you can see the information was accurate, but because of the inconsistency of how it was presented, it seemed as though she made up the story to fit the arena she was in at the time.

I helped her draft a one page bio and showed her how to cut it to fit the requirements of a shorter bio without changing the story. When you are asked for a bio you have 2 options, send your complete bio and tell the recipient to use as much or as little as they see fit or craft your own 50 word or less bio. If you choose to write your own shortened bio, make it similar to a mission statement and highlight what is important for the audience. Here is what I developed as her 50 word bio:

After living more than a decade in a progressively abusive marriage, Monica decided the safety of her children was her only priority. She gained the courage to escape her abusive marriage. As a survivor, she has made it her mission to empower and equip women with the resources to be victorious after abuse.

I know the immediate desire is to cite your accolades in your introduction/bio, but remember "added value" is what matters most. By sharing her experience instead of her credentials, it incites interest in what she has to say, with the belief that she would deliver a relatable message instead of rattling off statistics and case studies.

Again, it is important to know your audience and the nature of the event. For example, if she was being cited as an expert in the field of domestic violence to move a bill or get funding her 50 word bio would read as follows:

As a domestic abuse survivor, Monica earned a Masters in Psychology and is serving as director of "said agency" for the past 5 years, with a 76% success rate of helping women rebuild their lives. She has raised an excess of $1.3M for families in need.

Although the bios differ in reflecting what she has done and why she has chosen to do it, they both are simply snapshots modified to reach her target audience and add validity to her knowledge of the subject matter. She has the opportunity to build rather than explain from either point. If I was able to discover this information about her online, how many other people searched and found the same information? I will address social media and your online reputation in a later chapter because it is such broad topic.

This is not a book on resume writing but what I can tell you is your resume should be a snapshot of accomplishments rather than a chronological list of tasks. Certain skill sets are required for a position whether it's an accountant or a technical analyst. So if your resume says, *"I processed this, paid that, managed that,"* so did the other 100 people that submitted their resumes. They key is to talk about what was the result of your responsibilities and tasks.

You can promote your personal brand and build your resume by taking initiative and offering possible solutions. Bosses and clients alike aren't interested in complaints. They need possible solutions. When you take initiative it gives the impression that you are genuinely concerned.

Recently, I worked with a project manager that was upset because one of his teammates wasn't carrying her weight. He complained to the department manager and was disappointed that his manager did not fire the slacking co-worker. He even said, "Why should I be a superstar when she gets to do nothing?"

As I coached him, the first question I asked was, "Are you looking to get her fired? Or, are you campaigning for a promotion?" Of course he answered, "I am looking to get promoted, but she needs to be fired too." "Yes," I chuckled to myself.

I had him identify the tasks that she was responsible for that he could easily take over. Once he discovered which responsibilities he could seamlessly assume, I told him to present his idea to the manager. I told him to find a way of saying,

"I know with all the organizational changes, Susie may become a little overwhelmed. What do you think about me assuming this part of her workload, that way she can focus on her new duties?"

I thought that was a simple way of explaining his next steps, but he looked a little confused about the approach. I explained to him that once he complained he was not only bashing his co-worker, he came across as a "know it all." By offering a suggestion not only is he allowing his manager to remain in a position of power, he is showing his manager that he has initiative and the success of the team in mind. With a solution rather than a complaint, he was able to showcase his critical thinking skills and display his added value.

It's never a good thing to point out the deficiencies of someone else instead of displaying your credentials, experience and willingness to help. Believe it or not someone else being substandard does not always equate to you being above standard. Always remember it is about the "added value." Not greater than or less than.

Willingness to help demonstrates the characteristics of a leader and gives the impression that the success of the team and organization is as important as your success. I am proud to say that this gentleman later became a senior project manager, leading his team to implement three times as many projects as the previous year. Talk about a resume builder.

Now this gentleman is able to say, "As a Senior Project Manager I led a team of 6 project managers to implement three times the number of projects than the previous year which decreased the project turnaround time by 67%." I can assure you this scenario would have went a different direction had he thrown his co-worker under the bus.

If you are a creative person like an artist, author, photographer and have a portfolio in lieu of or to compliment your resume, this is your opportunity to WOW perspective clients and employers. As a creative person, there is more flexibility in how you present your work. For example, if you are a graphic designer, instead of showing something that you've created, show the finished product. If you designed a book cover, show a copy of the actual book not just the design. Not only will it display your ingenuity, but also demonstrate creative uses for your designs. To take it a step further it shows that you are capable of designing to meet the project requirements while maintaining brand integrity.

As a designer it is also important to display the diversity of your work. Don't limit your portfolio to one medium. Have a balance of both digital and print designs. The competition is fierce, and as I said earlier you are not always competing on a local level, your competition may be global.

Just like anything else, in this age of technology, it is good to have an online as well as a tangible portfolio. A client or employer may ask you to provide him or her with your portfolio; it's a lot easier and less expensive to send a link rather than deliver it in person or via mail when it's not necessary.

It's not too often that we get to the center stage role so make every moment count! Your resume, portfolio and bio are the prelude to you and a representation of your brand so it is important to have it available at all times. Timing is everything. If you are prepared, you don't have to get ready and sacrifice your brand or an opportunity.

You may be the best at what you do, but people may not know who you are. It is important to be visible and memorable. Never forget, there is a difference between seeking attention and being visible. Everything you say, do, wear, produce and reside in reflects your personal brand.

NOTES

NOTES

Social Media

The very thought of social media may make some of you cringe, while others may feel that this chapter can easily be skipped because you believe that you have gotten this beast called social media by the horns. Whatever your feelings may be about social media, I encourage you to keep reading. I can guarantee that you will discover things that you are doing that may be hurting your brand or learn more ways to gain exposure for your brand.

Social media is ruled by relevant, real-time information and content that is engaging. I could easily write an entire book on personal branding with the use of social media. Instead I will give you a quick snapshot into the pitfalls and peaks of branding yourself through social media. Because social media evolves daily thanks to the innovative minds of the new generation, it is important to arm yourself with a few foundational techniques that will help you succeed no matter how information technology platforms evolve. Whether you accept it or not, we live in a technology driven world.

First, I am going to explore some basic principles that are applicable to both the employee as well as the entrepreneur. Then I will make a more in depth exploration geared towards the entrepreneur. But, I strongly suggest that employees begin to view their personal brand as a business. The business is YOU!

What exactly is social media? In the beginning, social networking was simply a tool that our children, Generation X and Nexters used to keep in touch. What originally began as a way to keep in contact with friends and the latest celebrity gossip quickly evolved into the most utilized form of communication.

More business is conducted via handheld devices than with a handshake.

With globalization and "real time" information, social media has become a very necessary evil. With camera phones and video apps, events are documented and reported as they happen. The world has become a mobile society. When we think of "social media" the names Facebook, LinkedIn, Twitter, etc. are top of mind, but it extends beyond those platforms. Social media is defined as *any and all online interaction, creation or exchange online.* Yes, that includes blogs, websites, online portfolios, internet radio, podcasts and even online surveys.

The internet has become a source for entertainment, information, and connection. People use the internet for almost everything these days. Whether it's to catch up on sports scores during a commute or watching a how-to video to prepare a special dinner, people are attracted to the convenience and variety of online engagement. It only makes sense to be where people are looking and spending their time and money.

The way others see you online is how they will ultimately evaluate your personal brand and decide whether or not they will hire or contract with you. It is important that you shine as much positive light on you and your brand as possible, so learn to manage your online presence effectively.

You never know who is watching you or how they came to know of your existence. Don't put anything online that you wouldn't want a client, decision maker or the front-page of the newspaper to broadcast. I know that America is a free country and we possess the freedom of speech. But free speech can be costly. Instead of spending valuable time crafting an explanation of why something was said, some things are better left unspoken.

You don't have to become an online marketing expert to effectively manage how you want your personal brand to be viewed in cyberspace. The world has become very competitive; don't get overlooked because of a negative online presence or a lack of presence online.

It is important to monitor your personal brand online frequently. What you do on the web is equally important or even more important than how you are perceived in person. Whether you are applying for a job or you are a business owner, you should know what is being said about you or your business online.

It was become common for people to research information about you using a search engine than they are reviewing references. The information that is provided online, tells the story of who you are, what you are about, and what you do without a person ever meeting you. Your presence is no longer only physical you have an online footprint as well. Be careful where you step. "Googled" is now an official word in the dictionary. Get the hint? People are doing their due diligence more and more often.

Job Seekers/Employees

The days of searching the newspaper for the current job openings, then mailing or faxing your resume to apply are long gone. You were judged by the paper your resume was printed on, your credentials and every resume was reviewed. Those days are over. The process for applying for a job has received a complete overhaul.

Many organizations have minimized their human resources department by reducing and in some cases eliminating the number of recruiters on staff. A lot of companies have resorted to hiring a third party to source for candidates on their behalf. Thanks to keyword searches and hashtags, the internet has made cyberspace a prime source to discover candidates. With the current state of technology and the job market, candidates are being found without the candidate knowing that an open position exists.

In today's world people will Google you before they contact you. In some cases, your online reputation is all that a potential employer or client has to go on. Even if you are not looking at all for a position or just passively looking, social media can be your friend. You never know when your company will downsize and eliminate your position; it is advantageous if you are able to appear on recruiters' or headhunters' radar before you need them.

There is such a thing as social media etiquette and just like face to face interactions you have to be aware, courteous and mindful of the things you say and share. Here are a few tips to make sure that your online presence is attracting the people and clients to you.

Avoid Making Critical Comments

There is always some type of drama or heated discussion online about a political stance or what we are passionate about. We all have a position on one side or the other. There is nothing wrong with that. What I will say is don't let free speech cost you the deal or the job. It's human nature to say someone or something is bad rather than mention what makes the alternative good. As I stated earlier tearing someone else down will never make you look better. If you have an adverse opinion make sure you articulate it in an effective, respectable manner.

It is important to keep things in context. If you are a non-profit that supports victims of domestic abuse by all means you should post news, information, affirmations and your opinions about law changes. But, if you are a CPA trying to attract big corporate executives you may not want to voice your opinion about "greedy" executives.

Accept Friends and Invitations

The purpose of social media is to grow your network. How can you do that if you never accept invitations to connect from people that you don't know directly? Of course you have to exercise good judgment. If you review the person's profile and it conflicts with your personal brand, values, or truth, don't accept them. But, if there are no red flags connect with him or her. What do you have to lose?

I know several entrepreneurs and artists of varying types that have their online profiles blocked, private and hidden. This surprises me because the purpose of having an online presence is to extend your reach. It's not often that a random person tries to connect with you *just because*. They are usually seeking you out for a reason. You never know if that person "friending" you is a fan, promoter, or potential client. Use wisdom but never discount a person simply because you don't know them.

Avoid posting explicit pictures/pictures in uniform

Many people have been discovered because of their 15 minutes of fame in the media. By the same token, that same 15 minutes has also cost many people their livelihood. We work hard and have earned the right to play hard, but remember you have an image to maintain. It's not good to post pictures of yourself in uniform doing something questionable. I know you are thinking, "What I do on my own time is my business." If a company logo is displayed while you're doing it, it's no longer just your business. It's officially company business.

When you are on company time, wearing a company logo, on company property or in a company vehicle, the perception is that you are an agent of that organization and they reserve the right to terminate your employment if you are acting in a way that will discredit or defame the brand.

Companies are very sensitive about maintaining their brand integrity. There is a moral clause written into several celebrity endorsement contracts. Society has watched several athletes lose an endorsement because of something that he or she did in their personal life that conflicted with the moral values of the company that endorsed him or her.

The reason why companies are so protective of their brand integrity is because the brand is associated with an experience and companies do not want a negative thought to be associated with their brand.

Watch Grammar and Spelling

There is a constant battle over grammar and spelling when it comes to online writing. One side says it's just social media and you are communicating with people that are in your circle. If this interaction was in person formal English would not be used. Because we use our smartphones to engage in social media the need for shortcuts is one of convenience more than desire. That is true; however, there is a difference between formal English and good grammar. I ran across a post by a 40 year old woman going to school for some type of medical occupation that read:

"Wud up wit cha, dat shyt is hot"

Yes, that stunned me too! After you read that sentence a few times to understand it, what is your impression of its author? How likely is it that you would call her for an interview? If you saw this, how likely would it be that you would do business with her? I think it's safe to say that the general consensus is she would not make the cut.

We all make typos, use acronyms, and let's not forget autocorrect can be our enemy, but try to minimize the errors when possible especially if you are an entrepreneur or public figure. You never want to appear careless or that you lack attention to detail.

Be Courteous

Time and time again as children we were told to *mind our manners*. The bad news is that you are never too old to outgrow using your manners. It is important that you still operate with a certain level of professionalism when you are interacting with people online. You never know who that person is, who they may know and who is watching.

There are more effective ways to voice your opinion or point of view without the use of profanity or being disrespectful. You don't want to be labeled as a cyber-bully because you chose not to use your words effectively. There is a time and place for everything. If you have an issue or concern with someone, take it offline or at least away from the public eye.

Picture Perfect

When choosing a profile picture, always choose a professional picture or a picture that represents your brand. This means that your picture should be current and a correct representation of what you look like. No, this does not mean that you have to go and spend hundreds of dollars on professional headshots, but you may want to stay away from using the college picture of you and the beer bong, that bikini shot from the last girls' trip, or a picture that is 20 years old.

You know they say a picture is worth a thousand words. What does your picture say about you? What impression would a potential client or employer have if they were to see the pictures of you online? It's the first impression that becomes the lasting impression. I know you can't always judge a book with a single look, but that single look has to compel others to read the book.

No picture or a stock photo can be as damaging as a bad photo. If you don't have a profile picture and you are actively using social media, one may draw the conclusion that you have something to hide, that you don't follow through to completion. These assumptions may be far-fetched to you, but when you have recruiters and clients who are bombarded with sales pitches and resumes, they reserve the right to be selective.

Your face is sometimes considered the logo of you and/or your business online. Make sure that the photograph you are using as your profile picture reflects your professional image and is dressed how you would present yourself in person.

Fact or Fiction

We all have dreams, fantasies and sometimes delusions about who we are and what we desire to be. It is easy to create a new persona in cyberspace. Building an online persona that is not true can easily come back to bite you. What's a little fiction among friends? It's the difference between someone thinking you are a trustworthy source or a fabricator. Don't paint a picture perfect profile padded with false accolades and credentials.

When the truth discovered is instead of being told, it can have very damaging consequences. I once encountered a gentleman that presented himself to be something that he wasn't. According to him, he had clients worldwide and I should hire him because he was a hot commodity. He went as far as to pressure me into the sale by saying he was going to see a client in Germany for a couple of days. I thought that was odd considering the flight time and cost to Germany from the US is rather expensive so why go just for a "couple days?" I responded to him by saying,

"My daughter studied in Germany for a month, where are you going while you're there?" His story immediately changed when he perceived himself as being backed into a corner. I didn't want to come across as adversarial that is why I asked a question that the answer would expose him instead of directly telling him that he was lying.

You never know who knows who or what people know, so keep it honest and you won't need to come up with an excuse. People do business with people they know and trust. Don't try to give false information to close the sale and lose a client in the process.

Who's Who

While perusing online profiles, many people wonder how some people gained so many contacts and connections. The first thought may be that you need to collect them as well and try to launch an online collection drive. Resist the urge and don't do it!

There is a difference between a campaign and a collection drive. An online campaign is a strategic approach to create and cultivate relationships. A collection drive is the desire to gain online connections simply for the purpose of having them. The problem with collecting is that the focus is on gaining connections not actually connecting with them or connecting them.

It's important to know the rules and purpose of the social media platforms. For example, LinkedIn is a professional network. The audience is geared towards professionals that are seeking business opportunities and expanding their networks. If there is someone that you desire to connect with, send them an introduction message with your invitation. If you send the generic; they may be skeptical of your invitation and deny the connection. Give a person a reason to accept your invitation. Why should they connect with you in lieu of the thousands of other people that sent invitations?

Spam is never acceptable! Spam is to solicit someone to utilize your goods, services and or recommendation. You know those people that call your house during dinner trying to sell you something you don't need or want? That's you when you send an invitation or friend request to someone you don't know or don't have a real reason to connect with them.

Recently, someone sent me an invitation to connect with her on LinkedIn. As soon as I accepted her invitation she sent me a message that said she is looking to get writing jobs so could I post her link on my page and share it with my networks? I immediately removed her as a connection. Why? That was textbook spam. I have no idea who she is, what her books are about or if she is a good writer.

Even if I considered doing what she asked, she included no introduction about herself or her work. By simply sending me a link, she expected me to research what her writing was all about and craft an introduction about her and/or a synopsis of her book. When asking for something at least extend the courtesy of making it easy for people to say yes to you.

Privacy Settings

You can adjust the settings on your profile to be private or semi-private. You may want to do that if you choose to use social media as your platform to let off steam. But again, don't put anything online that you wouldn't want the people you do business with to see and/or read. Although you may opt not to connect with those people, it doesn't stop your personal friends from sharing your words and pictures.

I've discovered that the older I become, the smaller the world becomes. The six degrees of separation is being reduced to three or less. With globalization and the various social media platforms, people are connected easier and more often. Jobs are causing people to relocate and our families move away from where they were born which is extending of personal and professional networks.

On the different platforms you can select various privacy settings and choose what is shared. All of my profiles are public, but I choose not to share everything within my profile with everyone.

Here are a few things that both the employee and the entrepreneur can do that will attract the right clients and/or employers.

1. **Add keywords in your profile.** Adding a few keywords or words that a person would most likely search for in your profile will increase your chances of being discovered. It's important that you use words people would commonly use. For example, one of my clients is an *intimacy expert*. The common person would not search that term, but they would search *human sexuality* or *sex therapist*. This small addition will assist you in directing traffic to your profile.

2. **Develop a profile that makes others want to know you.** It's a little difficult for people to write about themselves and their accomplishments. There is not a template, but make sure that your profile is complete and includes your expertise, education, and experience when applicable. You may even get

creative and add a headline. Make sure that your profile picture is professional and eye catching.

3. **Don't ask people who don't really know your work for a testimonial or recommendation.** If the person doesn't really know you or your brand you will be left with a generic or less than favorable recommendation. It's better to have a few quality reviews or recommendations than several mediocre ones.

4. **Have a complete profile.** If you took the time to set up a profile, why not take a moment and fill it with content. When you leave your profile incomplete it can give the impression that you don't have follow through and you don't always do your best. It's completely acceptable to add links into your profile that lead to other social media platforms, articles, testimonials, or anything else that will help set you apart from the pack.

Entrepreneurs/Business Owners

For the employee an online presence is optional but for the entrepreneur, an online presence is essential. In addition to the section above, the entrepreneur has more work to do. You may have a successful personal presence online, but creating an online presence for your business is quite different.

For many people their personal and professional lives have become a true balancing act. The only way to keep things moving in tandem is to be mobile. Whether it's an app on their smartphone or the ability to conference call from the car, more and more people are mobile and convenience has become their "must have."

I don't want to insult your intelligence by addressing what an entrepreneur is. The word entrepreneur is not just limited to people that own an actual business that sells a good or service. If you are an author, speaker, artist, or a person that provides any type of goods or services to generate income, you are an entrepreneur. And, in that case, the business is you. As soon as you think of yourself as a profitable, successful business, building your brand will become intuitive.

Like I said earlier in this chapter, I could compose an entire book on social media and branding, but I'd rather focus on providing you with the foundational structure on how to build and maintain your brand by developing an online reputation. If you choose not to hire someone to manage your online campaign, make sure you pay attention to this chapter.

There are a couple of foundational concepts that I must address before I continue with the *how to* piece. Before you launch an online campaign, you have to possess a clear picture of who your target audience is, what you wish to accomplish and how you plan to measure your success. There are several templates on creating a marketing strategy. I strongly recommend that you find one and use it. You will thank me later.

Most people know they want a product or service that they can sell, and sell enough that they receive a steady stream of income. But, few people know who they want to sell to and why. Without knowing the *who* and the *why*, you will hit the ground running and run into a dead end because you don't have a clear direction.

Online Interaction

Branding your business online is not about presenting yourself to the world. That is advertising and promotion. Remember branding is about the experience! In order for you to create an experience, you have to engage with your audience. By engaging your audience, they will be willing to share, participate and buy whatever it is that you are providing. This can bring more interested viewers in that can also give their suggestions and opinions.

No matter how shy or modest a person appears to be, everyone desires their 15 minutes of fame. When you respond to your audience it shows that they are being recognized and that makes them feel good. By interacting online you will start building credibility for your business and your brand.

There is another reason for interacting with your fan base online. Interaction is part of the formula that algorithms use to determine your ranking. The goal is to appear in the news feeds as much as possible, whenever possible. The more you interact by posting content, the more people will like, share, retweet, recommend and repost your posts. Whether the feedback is good, bad, or neutral, respond in a timely manner and mind your manners. Unless a post or comment is downright derogatory, do not delete it, just respond accordingly. When you simply delete an unfavorable comment, it gives the appearance that you have something to hide.

A negative comment or situation spreads like wildfire online jeopardizing your reputation and brand. Sales can decline if you don't take concrete steps to resolve the matter as soon as possible. Have a strategy in place to counteract the negativity and help you respond as quickly as possible if anything negative arises online about your brand. Unfortunately, an unfavorable comment can be posted by anyone. Your clients, competition, and the general public are all "correspondents" online.

Handling negative or adverse online comments cannot be avoided, but it can be managed effectively. If someone posts a negative comment about you, respond to their post with a clarifying post on your own site or blog explaining the situation. Stand your ground and add a link to your own website or blog where the readers can find more information about you.

Once you provide your side of the story or response leave it alone. Avoid getting into petty online disputes by responding to the continuation of idle banter. Always make sure that you do not use harsh language. It will make the readers even more suspicious while you are busy countering a negative post.

When I first published, someone decided they wanted to launch an "I hate Deondriea campaign" to smear my name. After I vented to my friend privately about how I felt, I replied to the post in a professional manner, and ironically people I didn't know defended me against the post. I must admit I was surprised that the negativity fizzled out the same day. Imagine what would have happened if I would have engaged in an online battle? I didn't get sucked into continuously defending myself with a response or rebuttal. Be open, honest and transparent, it works wonders.

In building your personal brand it is essential that you listen effectively as you interact with your audience on and offline. The result of focusing on the people that interact with you is you find out what their likes and pain points are. Knowing what matters to the people you interact with will make it easy for you to market to potential and current customers effectively. But you have to listen and pay attention.

Recently, I was in one of my favorite stores buying a pair of jeans. The jeans that are carried in that store are rather pricey, but they are well worth the value. As the sales clerk was assisting me, I told her that her store was the only store that I bought jeans from because I have been unsuccessful in finding a brand that fits as well anywhere else. As I was trying on my jeans she brought me a shirt. I told her again,

"I don't buy shirts here because I don't have an issue finding shirts elsewhere; my challenge is finding jeans." After I left the dressing room, she greeted me with a sweater to pair with my jeans.

I repeated my original statement, but she kept insisting that I buy a top. The sales clerk didn't listen to me. I would have bought two pairs of jeans, but she was busy trying to up sell a shirt to me. When I said, *this is the only store where I can find jeans that fit,* I shared what my pain point was and that I found value the jeans.

When interacting with your audience, don't respond for the sake of responding, listen to hear what they need and value. By listening you will find that you will become a magnet instead of a fisherman. People will be attracted to you and you will not have to seek them out.

Content Marketing

There are several social media platforms that utilize a variety of mediums. Knowing what your ideal client looks like, the type of product/service that you are selling, and what you are willing to invest in, are all factors necessary in deciding which option works best for your brand. Content marketing includes videos, pictures, updates, and blog content. It is highly recommended that you use a few of these marketing strategies to promote your brand.

A simple podcast, webinar, audio or video sound bite can be the one thing that separates you from your competitors. If you catch the eye of potential clients, you have already captured their interest; now make the most of it. Social media sharing *is adding a social bookmark and sharing options* online to help your guests and followers share your content with their own networks. Linking your social media platforms will assist you in creating visibility and extending your online reach.

Online reputation management and social media

Your brand reputation online is becoming more critical every day. Since the initiation of social networking and the ability for anyone to post anything online for the world to see, managing your brand's reputation is vital in today's digital world.

By implementing an online reputation management strategy, you can help protect your online reputation from negative criticism and at the same time, help you build your credibility online. As more people get connected in cyberspace, having an online reputation management strategy is critical in achieving online marketing success.

Price should not be the only thing that distinguishes you from the competition.

Building your brand online is essential to creating the reputation of your business in the digital world and it helps the audience identify that your business is different from others. Branding can help your business forge a relationship with potential clients and convert current clients into brand advocates.

The online world is useful for businesses because it provides access to a wide audience. The internet can also help you reach target audiences much faster than traditional marketing efforts. If you are interested in brand exposure and exposing your business to thousands of people, it is important to be attentive to your online branding to ensure that the audience that you are targeting will want to be associated with your brand.

Online branding might include a sign, symbol, and design patterns or colors that reflect the brand integrity. Online branding promotes sales and loyalty because clients can decide whether the business will fulfill their needs.

Before you begin an online campaign, you have to make sure your ducks are in a row or at least in the same pond. You have to start with basic questions to clarify your direction.

What would you like your brand to represent?

____

____

____

What image would you like the client to associate with your brand?

____

____

____

Online branding adds a personal touch to your business, and it is something that your audience can relate to. A successful online brand should always foster a positive feeling within the client to make them feel good about the decision that they are going to make. Your brand should assure your client of the value of the quality products and services that you provide and that it is worth the financial investment.

Online you will find hundreds of social media platforms that rely heavily on the participation of their network to supply them with content. When creating your brand profile make sure to add achievements, testimonials, press releases, and success stories, on various social media channels and article directories to spread your positive footprint online.

Start building an active community on the social media platforms and participate regularly in the discussions going on within your networks. You can use social media marketing to help spread your news and to formulate a good strategy to create more brand exposure for your company online. Your reputation may be your most valuable asset online. When people are looking for information, they usually turn to the search engines for answers. Someone in passing may use cyberspace to learn more about you to connect with you. Just for grins, you may want to look up your brand (yourself or business) online to see what the buzz is about.

Blogging

Blogging is sometimes considered to be the heart and soul of social media and should be included in every social media marketing campaign. Blogging *is a contraction of the* words **web log** *and is a discussion or information published online.* A blog can appear on a website, a blogsite, or other social media platforms.

There are two great things about blogging: you can choose the frequency, whether several times a day, daily, and several times a week; and what I personally love about blogging is the content can be repurposed. You can take snippets of the content from your blog and use it as posts for other social media platforms and you always have the option to link the other posts back to your blog.

It is a great idea to create a blog about your area of expertise. Use your blog to establish yourself as a subject matter expert without overtly promoting yourself. Once you create a new blog post, share it to your other social media profiles. If you continuously post relevant and engaging content, eventually you will build a loyal following of readers that will share your blog with their networks.

It is advantageous to utilize all of the benefits that a blog offers and optimize all of your blog posts. The best way to optimize your blog posts is by developing keyword rich content to generate organic search engine rankings.

Whether you are looking for a job or just marketing your company online, the bottom line is that you should build your name online so that you can be seen as the leader in your industry.

I always advise those who want to have a social media presence to think carefully about their intentions and objectives before opening an online account. Why? Because the moment you start, you have to continue. Consistency is what will attract people to you and keep them coming back again and again. Challenge yourself to think about what your goals are and what you are capable of delivering to the communities you serve in and outside of the marketplace.

LinkedIn

Creating a LinkedIn profile and ensuring that it is complete is a great way to promote your brand. LinkedIn allows you to connect with other professionals in every industry imaginable. One of the benefits on LinkedIn is its searchable without the use of hash tags. By using keywords in your profile, it will be easy for people to locate you and it will also help you to get personal rankings on the search engines.

Adding keywords to your profile is a very powerful tool that most people overlook. To effectively use keywords in your profile, create a list of keywords you are using to promote your business. Review your profile and insert those words everywhere that it's appropriate. The best section of your profile to pad with keywords is your professional summary. Because, the summary is at the top of your profile, it is easily accessible to entice people to continue reading, versus the task of muddling through your entire profile to discover your hidden gems.

Under no circumstances is it a good idea to SPAM!!! LinkedIn is not designed to for solicitors. If you have a complete profile and updates with useful content, prospective clients and/or employers will find you. Foster relationships with people as I described in the chapter about network. The same principles apply when social networking. Join the groups on LinkedIn that interested and actively engage with the other members do go in trying the sell. When people value what you have to say, they will seek you out.

I'm an advocate of making sure your LinkedIn profile including your professional experience and expertise. A complete profile will increase potential clients, employers and other essential people to locate you: it will also help you find the people that you need. Personally, I have used LinkedIn to find graphic designers, copy editors and more.

If you took the time to create a LinkedIn profile, ensure that it works to your advantage. As I stated in an earlier chapter, being visible is the most effective way to build your brand. By adding the companies that you have worked for in the past, you have the option to enable their logo on your profile. By adding in the company logo to your profile will increase your credibility as well as improve your visibility. Your name will appear in the search results for that company, giving you effortless exposure.

Facebook

To assist in improving your ranking on search engines, a Facebook profile is necessary. It is important to keep your profile updated with content that is relevant to you/your business. If you are using Facebook to communicate personally with your friends and family, create another account that focuses only on your business. Your Facebook fanpage should be handled differently than your personal page. Although you may receive several likes and comments on your personal page, that same content may not receive the same interest from your business audience.

With any online platforms, it is important that you be authentic, relevant and engaging. Yes, it's nice to share a few personal things about yourself in order to relate to your audience but not so much that that your audience pool deems your content irrelevant.

It is important that you add as many fields as you can on your profile to make it clear what type of business you have and the services that you offer.

Responsiveness is a key component in keeping your fan base engaged. If someone leaves a comment, don't just like the comment, say something back to them. By interacting with your audience people will continue to be engaged. The higher your page engagement is, the more often it will show up in the newsfeed of your followers, which will expose you to their *friends* and entice them to follow you as well.

Twitter

Twitter is the social media platform that people often overlook as a useful tool to build their personal brand. Having a presence on Twitter, it's easy to establish yourself as an authority in your industry and share relevant content with the world not just your followers.

Through the use of the *lists* and hashtag features, it is easy for potential clients and/or employers to locate you based on their area(s) of interest. When I first joined Twitter I started following my competitors and people who I thought were change leaders in my field. I chose to follow those people to see what was and was not working, to retweet him or her, and to build a firm foundational presence. This can help you get on the map where others can follow you, so that you can start building your own network.

The same rules apply on Twitter as the other social media platforms. The need for a complete profile is a priority. Avoid making sales pitches on your profile. Instead add something funny or interesting, which will compel others to connect with you. The great thing about Twitter, is the limited character availability simply gives your audience sound bites, which will lead followers to your website or connect with you on other platforms to gain more information about you and/or your products and services. Think of Twitter as an appetizer before the meal.

Add files and links

One of the best features about an online campaign is you can incorporate your print media as well. There are features that will allow you to add links and documents, photos, videos and more into your profile and/or website. By adding these items potential clients have the opportunity to review what you have to offer prior to contacting you. This will enhance your profile while building credibility.

Share, Retweet and Comment

Personal branding is not about self-promotion, it's about adding value. You add value by what you say, do and produce. In order to provide value, you have to know what matters to your audience. Do not hesitate to follow the conversations that your target audience is having. Of course I cannot go into all the details of what to watch for in this book without making it overwhelmingly lengthy. Instead, I encourage people to attend one of my live events to better mine the information that you are looking for without the assistance of keyword searches.

There is a fear that sharing, tweeting, or commenting on someone else's post will promote the other person. In actuality this gives you visibility. When you comment of someone's posts you are immediately given access to their fan base. That alone should have you jumping for joy.

I cannot tell you how many clients I have attracted by a discussion thread on someone else's page. I never said like, promote and share my page. My response alone was enough to incite people to want to know more about me and/or what I have to say.

When you retweet someone generally, they will in turn follow you. When their followers see that they are following you they eventually will follow you too. The more your name appears in the news feed, the more visibility your brand will gain.

When using social media to provide links relating to your niche, follow leaders within that field and those within the local scene, contribute to discussions, and interact with people. People won't know you if you keep to yourself, so take the first step and interact; most people won't mind, some are happy to continue the conversation.

Social media is a vehicle for communicating online. Using social media platforms is an excellent method for personal branding. If used correctly you will be visible and attract your ideal clients instead of having to mine for them.

There is so much to this game called social media. I could easily devote an entire book on each one of the platforms. Instead, I often host webinars and workshops that will help you master the world of social media and leverage each platform effectively.

NOTES

NOTES

Rebranding

What happens when you find yourself in a holding pattern at work or your business sales have flat lined? The knee jerk reaction is to rebrand, recreate or reintroduce your brand or product. Rebranding may or may not always be the best course of action.

Rebranding *is an approach in which a new name, value proposition, designs, or combination thereof is created for an established brand with the purpose of developing a new, distinguished identity for the intended audience.* Rebranding usually includes, but is not limited to changes to a brand's logo, name, image, and marketing strategy. These changes are usually to reposition the brand for advancement or opportunity.

Rebranding may be necessary to remain relevant. Internal or external factors may influence the need to expand, reposition or revitalize your brand.

Is the goal of rebranding a stepping stone or a milestone?

When beginning the rebranding process, it is a good idea to determine if the focus of the brand is evolutionary or revolutionary. The evolutionary purpose of rebranding is the message has become stale or you are evolving to keep your brand relevant. If the approach is revolutionary it simply means somehow you diverted from your original goals and objectives and you have to reestablish your brand identity.

The goals for every brand are to promise value that the target audience will embrace and create a call to action. With worldwide access via the web and technology, the marketplace is saturated with choices, leaving consumers more aware of their choices. In order to create brand loyalty and distinguish yourself in the marketplace or the workplace your promises of value must be delivered.

The goal of rebranding is to create a brand that is better than before. Because rebranding requires such a huge commitment and creates an impact a methodical implementation process should be followed. This involves a strategy and positive, memorable interactions that will foster trust between your brand and the audience to improve and/or change their perception of you. A check point in the planning process is to ask yourself:

How does the marketplace perceive you?

____

____

____

____

How do you want the marketplace to perceive you?

____

____

____

____

And if those are different, how are you going to change it?

____

____

____

____

A successful campaign requires more than a revamped logo and upgraded promotional material. It requires a vision that will convince existing clients and stakeholders to see and perceive you differently.

Year after year we make resolutions that usually fizzle out before the month of January is over. When it comes to personal branding you can't haphazardly rebrand yourself because you're motivated or simply want a change. Rebranding without research defeats the purpose of branding. It is important that you know what you are getting yourself into and why.

There are a few clarifying questions that will ensure whether or not rebranding is necessary. If rebranding is required you have to make sure that you are heading in the right direction. If you simply take off running without a plan, you are bound to return to this place you are at again.

Why do you think you need to rebrand yourself?

____

____

____

____

Rebranding yourself is not something you do because you are simply "looking for a change." Change is not better or worse it's just an inevitable constant. There is always the option to change without growth, but it's difficult to grow without changing. You have to envision what you want the end result to look like and create a strategy that will get you there.

What problem are you looking to resolve?

____

____

____

____

The problem that you are looking to resolve may not have anything to do with your brand. It may be that you need to review your options and take advantage of opportunities. A lot of times we expect to be chosen but never threw our hat into the ring. You may be excellent or even the best at what you do, but your manager may be unaware of your desire to obtain a role in leadership.

Has your current brand limited your growth potential?

____

____

____

____

If your brand has limited your growth potential, take the time to assess why and how you have been limited. Do you need to change how you present yourself or the work that you produce? Are there additional skills that you need to acquire? Has the industry that you work in declined? Are you able to provide the same value in another industry? These are some of the questions that you should consider when comparing your brand and your growth.

Have you been pigeonholed with a certain brand?

What message do you want to convey? To whom?

Is your brand associated with something that is no longer significant?

Is your brand out of synch with your current needs and desires?

____

____

____

____

When making the decision to rebrand yourself, consider the long term goal. What you do today will impact tomorrow's outcome. Consider your position, industry, professional, personal and financial goals and decide:

Will this solution work 10 years from now based on what you can anticipate?

____

____

____

____

As you begin the branding process, there are a few items that you may want to add to your knowledge arsenal to ensure that the rebranding strategy is successful. Your brand is a culture; it's your value that embodies everything from your message, methods, and the customer experience. So don't think that changing your "look" is enough to accomplish your goals, unless it is your look that has impeded your growth.

Everyone has an opinion about what you should be doing and how. We value the people that are in our lives but you can't brand or rebrand by committee. If you allow too many people to influence you on what your brand will be it will only delay the outcome and divert the focus of the goal. This is when it's essential to bring in your business coach or mentor that will help you to objectively create a branding strategy. Only include the most essential people in the decision making process. Putting the wrong person in charge may become costly in terms of time and other resources.

If you are sincerely considering rebranding yourself, it is advisable to consult a business coach, mentor or a professional to ensure that you are in alignment with your objectives and goals. Don't be afraid to see what your competition is doing. The goal is not to replicate them but to spark your own ideas. You do not have to recreate the wheel, just learn to steer it effectively.

NOTES

NOTES

NOTES

Be You!

If you could choose to be anyone in the world, you should always choose to be YOU! I hate to break the news to you but there is only one Oprah Winfrey, John F. Kennedy, and Michael Jordan and there will only be one YOU. Just like all the trailblazers and the iconic brands we idealize, they set out to be the best that they knew how to be. They were able to impact business and society by doing what they were supposed to do! These aforementioned people are successful because they believed in who they were, what made them unique and how they could impact the world around them.

I could offer you a bunch of clichés, quotes, scriptures, jokes or old wives tales about being you instead someone else, but reality is, they are useless gifts unless you first know who you are. Until you discover who you are, you will never know what you are supposed to be or what you are supposed to do.

> *Above all you should not be what you do,*
> *but what you do should be who you are!*

Every interaction is an interview to be hired, promoted, or recognized. Consider both the long term and short term consequences of your actions as well as the opportunities you choose to do or don't do. Your personal brand takes time and attention to build, but one careless or whimsical act can destroy it in seconds. Proof of how a single indiscretion can destroy the most well recognized brands is prevalent in daily headlines or online posts.

The responsibility of being your brand becomes a natural and instinctual part of who you are. You must possess the mindset and personal accountability when you decide to define, live and manage your personal brand. Every day you realize that you are required to meet certain standards that you have established for both yourself and the communities in which you live, work and serve.

Every time you are in a meeting, conference, online, at a networking reception or other event, you should be mindful of what others are experiencing about you and what you want others to experience about you. Public interactions are just like interviews, you are being evaluated by the audience. When you begin to view yourself as a brand, your perspective will transform and you will become more mindful about how you approach the personal brand you are defining and fostering.

We all have gifts, talents, and skills. Don't be afraid to build on your strengths to capitalize on them. A wise person knows both their strengths and weaknesses. Knowing both will assist you in moving your brand forward. You have to know and live in your own truth. Never let anyone label you or define who you are.

It is what you do every day that determines your personal brand. Consistency and congruency has to be found in everything you say, do and produce. You should know what you want others to feel, think and experience when they are exposed to you and/or your work.

What are you willing to give?

What do you desire to gain?

It is human nature to want to hear things that makes us feel good. We love it when our name is called, but with that, you have to be able to accept criticism and feedback. I personally don't believe there is such a thing as constructive criticism because it is all about perception. The message has to pass through the filter of the person receiving criticism. Depending on what is said, when it's said, how it was said and by whom it was said, a decision is made whether the criticism is constructive.

There is something inspiring about seeing and hearing people cheer for us. But beware of filling the stands with cheerleaders because they cheer whether you win or lose. It is important that you have at least one truth teller in the bleachers. A truth teller is *a person that has a vested interest in your success*. A truth teller is a person you trust who will tell you what you need to know not what you want to hear. The person that you designate as your truth teller may hurt your feelings, but will always have your best interest at heart. Remember it's a person that cares about you that will tell you when you stink.

A truth teller may often have a contrary opinion and you may perceive this person as a "hater." But in actuality this is the person who is looking at things objectively. When he or she provides you with a critique or criticism, they will always provide a reason and an alternative point of view to build you up because their desire is to see that you are successful.

Several years ago, while I was working at my church as an administrator, the church's graphic designer created a new letterhead. It was my responsibility to have the letterhead printed. When I presented the design to my printer she said,

"In good conscience, I will not print this. If you want to be taken seriously, church or not, you won't be."

Talk about a gut punch! I thought the letterhead was cute. My printer quickly pointed out that the design was cute, but not professional. She explained to me what was wrong with the design. Although I understood what she was saying and thought it was very valuable feedback, the graphic designer was not too thrilled at having her design kicked back.

I had a relationship with my printer so I trusted her professional opinion, but because the graphic artist did not have a relationship with her, she did not value the opinion of the printer. If you receive legitimate criticism, then you should take it as feedback and make your work better.

The buzz word these days is hater! People these days seem to be more consumed with who is *hating* on them instead of who loves them and why. Know more about who you are or what you do. Everyone will never love you and you will always have critics.

Contrary to popular belief haters are valuable. Here are a few ways to use haters effectively.

- **Haters will cause you to check yourself-***because critics or haters look for what's wrong, they actually help you trouble shoot your campaign, service, idea or goods free of charge.* They will point out things that you may not have thought about. We all need that periodic checkout.

- **Haters make good PR representatives-***Believe it or not sometimes bad press it better than no press at all.*

Critics or haters will talk about you to anyone that will listen, which will cause people to want to know more about you, your product or services.

There will always be people and situations to discourage you, but if you know who you are and what you should be doing these minor distractions will not be a distraction for you. It's up to you if you choose to allow those things to be stepping stones or building blocks.

In order for you to build a personal brand it's totally acceptable for you to have a coach, cheerleader and critic. You will find that each one brings a different value to your brand. Don't run away from the critics; just learn to use them more effectively.

Remember I said every *interaction is an interview*. No matter where you are and what you are doing, be the brand that YOU want others to see, believe in and recommend.

Now that we have gone over every aspect of what it takes to build your personal brand, it's time to get organized. It is important that you have a plan in place to build your brand on and offline. Make sure you know what you want your brand to be known for. You have to determine what look, feel and word you want to be synonymous with. Above all you have to know what you are willing to commit to. If you know you aren't very computer savvy or are not in a position to hire someone, don't launch an online campaign that requires interaction and a lot of your attention.

Don't just be who you are, own it! I met a woman whose tagline on her business card read, *"I make shit happen."* That was a bold move on her part and she owned that. She always received one of two reactions, either people were offended and chose not to do business with her or others admired her confidence and were drawn to her. Whatever the outcome was, she was prepared to deal with it. She was willing to risk offense to allow potential clients to disqualify themselves. With such a bold tagline people knew right away if they wanted to do business with her.

Someone else will brand you, if you don't do it yourself. You may not like the brand that they choose for you. It will take a lot of time and resources to rebrand yourself, so why not do it coming out of the gate. You never want to be judged by popular opinion, especially if you have not influenced that opinion.

Consistency is KEY! I have said it several times throughout this book because it is above all the most essential element for building, fostering and maintaining your brand. You have to persistently keep your face, name, work and expertise in the forefront of the minds of the people that you are trying to reach in order to become an industry leader or expert in your field.

When you think about the brands that you support, are you buying a product or an experience? There are certain places that I shop simply because they provide the goods that I need at a reasonable price and I don't expect quality customer service. On the other hand, there are places that I shop solely because of the experience. As far as I'm concerned they could sell widgets and I would purchase them solely because of the buying experience. The product or experience has to be the focus when promoting your brand.

Perception is Reality

Who you are may not be how you appear to others. My mother used to say, *"Everybody ain't telling the same lie on you."* If you are consistently receiving feedback that is contrary to what you desire it to be, you may want to reexamine your actions and words. If no one has given you adverse feedback, it's a good idea to periodically do a self-check to ensure that you are in alignment with your brand identity.

What do people miss about you that they should know?

Personally, it seemed that everyone I met had the same opinion of me when they first met me. They thought I was a mean, uptight, stick in the mud. That is far from who I am and strive to be. But I had to check what I was doing that gave others that impression of me. When it comes to business I am focused and direct. When I entered a meeting I didn't indulge in small talk. To be candid, I am not a person that likes to attend meetings. Tell me what I need to know and I will properly execute it. To others, my actions made them feel like I was unapproachable.

Once I realized how much my actions impacted others, I made a few adjustments. I didn't change who I was, but I changed how I presented myself. I made sure I arrived a little early and chatted with the attendees, then when it was time to begin the meeting I said,

"Time to put our game faces on and get to work."

That minor adjustment made a world of difference and that difference ultimately made a difference in the outcome of the meeting. I found that people around the table were more engaged and open to what I had to say. They no longer viewed me as an adversary.

With the rise of social media, it's easy to lose sight of what your brand is all about. The person that you appear to be online is the same person that people expect to meet in person. It is important that you are always authentic, be who you are and know your truth. It's simple to create an online persona, but eventually you will have come from behind the computer and be YOU!

Navigating without a plan will not result in a successful personal brand strategy. Effective brand recognition requires focus, commitment and consistency that include information analytics, objectives, resources and timeframes. There has to be an implementation plan, but it should be flexible.

Being authentic is very important. People would prefer the real you rather than a replica of who you think they want. Being authentic is the first step to managing your brand. When you are authentic, being the best you that you can be comes naturally and you never have to worry about being caught off guard. Be aware of what people perceive you to be, because even though it may not be a reality for you at times, it is a reality for them all the time.

Make sure you are unforgettable by being YOU! What works for another person may not be your ticket, but find what works for you. I attended an event where everyone in the room had to give an introduction. Everyone stated their name, title, and why they were there. As the 30th and final person, I had to endure the repetitive pain of the pretense, "My name is and I'm a…" When it was my turn, I stood up and said,

"My name is Deondriea and I'm an alcoholic. Damn it, I hate when that happens, wrong meeting, just kidding. My name is Deondriea and I am a marketing manager."

After a few quick gasps and silence, laughter filled the room. By invoking such abstract humor in my introduction, I became one of the most memorable members of the group. Whether its humor, useless facts, or phenomenal anecdotes, find what makes you unique and stand out from the crowd.

When you are in tuned with yourself, confident in your abilities and accountable for your actions, you will find that being yourself is the best brand to wear!

Whether branding or rebranding yourself, continue to foster and allow your brand to evolve. This will keep your brand relevant and top of mind. Your personal brand must always represent an unapologetic, authentic you. Lastly, now that you know *what you want to be when you grow up,* you have to be able to quantify that into a marketable, valuable, and sustainable brand that is ready for primetime.

"Don't try to meet the standard, strive to set the precedence"-Deondriea Cantrice

Be Unapologetically YOU!!!

NOTES

NOTES

135

About the Author

As a dynamic speaker and celebrated author, Deondriea Cantrice has impacted many multifaceted audiences throughout the country with her life-changing message. She expertly entertains, educates, and inspires any  audience with her tales of true life to keep them engaged and motivated.

Audiences connect with Deondriea through her vivacious, interactive style, and approachable manner. She incorporates into her presentations the skills she gained from many years of experience in the communications industry and being certified in Six Sigma Green Belt, customer service training, and stress and time management. Deondriea is a highly sought after speaker because of her special talent for easily connecting with her audience, creating immediate feelings of trust and integrity.

She is the author of several books, including *Rhythm Can't Keep Time, Sometimes Love Just Ain't Enough; When Emotions Lie; You! Branding Yourself for Success; Tiptoes, Steel-Toes and Stilettos;* and *Write and Grow Rich*. She has been named as a finalist for the ***Stiletto Woman in Business Award (SWIBA) for the 2014 Author of the Year***.

After the Rain is more than just a journal; it's a transformative guide leading you towards reigniting passion and uncovering purpose. Through powerful affirmations, introspective reflections, and purposeful goal setting, embark on a journey to rebuild, reimagine, and revitalize your narrative. Purchase your copy today!

> **That personal touch is what we need at times!**

Attending a *You! Branding Yourself for Success* webinar or *LIVE* event is the key that you need to unlock the barriers of your personal brand. As a successful brand architect, Deondriea will equip you with the necessary tools to help you build and foster a sustainable personal brand!

You will learn:
How to maintain brand integrity!
Foster your brand through networking!
How to extend your brand's online reach!

To schedule Deondriea to facilitate a workshop with your team or to attend one of her upcoming events visit **www.deondriea.com**

EMPOWER YOURSELF

TO STAY MOTIVATED!

Motivation is not a euphoric drug that is to be administered in periodic doses, nor is inspiration a feeling; it is a call to action! When you are truly inspired, you will respond, act and move ahead. You will do whatever it takes despite how you feel or what you read.

Tiptoes, Steel-Toes and Stilettos is not your typical book of inspiration that delivers melodramatic lip service. It is a book filled with motivational quotes, inspirational anecdotes, and empowering affirmations that will stimulate you to take action by igniting your intrinsic fire.

Let's put your best foot forward to achieving your personal goals!

Access Granted recognizes the significance of self-care in building and maintaining confidence. The book offers self-care practices and emphasizes the need for self-compassion, setting boundaries, and prioritizing your own well-being as essential components of confidence cultivation. With its comprehensive exploration of confidence, backed by personal anecdotes and relatable examples, Access Granted serves as a guidebook for listeners seeking to unlock their true potential and access the life they desire. Purchase your copy today!

Let's Get Social!
Connect with Deondriea online!

@deondriea

@deondriea

@deondriea

@deondriea

@deondriea

@deondriea